The Book of Revelation
Unlocked

An Easy-to-Understand Walk Through the Bible's Final Message

Blessings!
Judy Woodward Bates
Mt. 6:33

Judy Woodward Bates

Cover Images: © depositphotos.com/c_lollok (blue cloth frame), © depositphotos.com/c-sashkin7 (key), © Licensed purchased image Dreamstime (Bible page)
Cover Design & Publishing assistant: The Author's Mentor,
www.TheAuthorsMentor.com

Scripture quotations marked (NASB®) are from the New American Standard Bible®, Copyright © 1960, 1971, 1977, 1995, 2020 by The Lockman Foundation. Used by permission. All rights reserved. www.lockman.org. Scripture quotations marked (NLT) are taken from the Holy Bible, New Living Translation, copyright ©1996, 2004, 2015 by Tyndale House Foundation. Used by permission of Tyndale House Publishers, Carol Stream, Illinois 60188. All rights reserved. Scripture quotations marked (NIV) are taken from the Holy Bible, New International Version®, NIV®. Copyright © 1973, 1978, 1984, 2011 by Biblica, Inc.™ Used by permission of Zondervan. All rights reserved worldwide. www.zondervan.comThe "NIV" and "New International Version" are trademarks registered in the United States Patent and Trademark Office by Biblica, Inc.™ Scripture quotations marked (ESV) are taken from The Holy Bible, English Standard Version® (ESV®), Copyright © 2001 by Crossway, a publishing ministry of Good News Publishers. All rights reserved. Scriptures marked CEV are taken from the CONTEMPORARY ENGLISH VERSION (CEV), Scripture taken from the CONTEMPORARY ENGLISH VERSION copyright© 1995 by the American Bible Society. Used by permission. Scriptures marked HCSB are taken from the HOLMAN CHRISTIAN STANDARD BIBLE (HCSB): Scripture taken from the HOLMAN CHRISTIAN STANDARD BIBLE, copyright© 1999, 2000, 2002, 2003 by Holman Bible Publishers, Nashville Tennessee. All rights reserved. Scriptures marked KJV are taken from the KING JAMES VERSION (KJV): KING JAMES VERSION, public domain. Scriptures marked (BSB) are taken from The Holy Bible, Berean Study Bible, Copyright ©2016, 2018 by Bible Hub, Used by Permission. All Rights Reserved Worldwide. Scriptures marked (GNT) are taken from The Good News Bible © 1994 published by the Bible Societies/HarperCollins Publishers Ltd UK, Good News Bible© American Bible Society 1966, 1971, 1976, 1992. Used with permission. Scripture marked (BLB) is quoted from the BlueLetterBible.org. All rights reserved.

Bargainomics Publications
ISBN-13: 978-0-9766166-3-4
Also available in eBook Publication.

PUBLISHED IN THE UNITED STATES OF AMERICA

Acknowledgments

I owe so many "thank yous" to the people who have helped turn this study into the book you now hold in your hands. Thank you to all my readers who have commented, encouraged, and questioned. You've led me to get this book assembled and to rewrite where better clarification was needed. Thank you to my husband Larry who has tirelessly discussed, read, and re-read all of this study with me.

A huge "Thank you!" to my pastor, Dr. Kevin Hamm, and to Phil Jones, my church's Minister of Pastoral Care, for taking time from their always overloaded schedules to read and critique the manuscript that became this book. Larry and I and all of Gardendale First Baptist are beyond blessed to have such a humble servant of God as Pastor Kevin as our under-shepherd and to have a dedicated staff member like Bro. Phil on our team.

I truly don't believe I would be at this point in my Christian walk without the teaching, encouragement, and friendship of my friend and former pastor, Dr. Clay Hallmark Jr. He, like Pastor Kevin, is a dedicated worker in the Kingdom, currently serving as senior pastor of First Baptist Church in Lexington, Tennessee. Thank you from the depths of my heart for your willingness to help with this project.

Lastly, a huge THANK YOU to Sammie Barstow, the best friend and editor I could ever have. She has saved me from the errors of my writing on more occasions than I can count and made me a far better writer than I could ever have been without her.

Resources

Resources for this study came from a variety of places, including, but not limited to, commentaries and writings by Adam Clarke, Henry Ward Beecher, John Trapp, John Walvoord, Charles Spurgeon, as well as my personal notes from sermons by Dr. Cecil Sewell and Dr. R. B. Culbreth.

Day 44 includes a quotation from Word Music. Day 63 relates an event heard on Dr. James Dobson's "Focus on the Family" radio program. Day 79 includes a portion of Don Moen's "God Will Make a Way."

All scriptures are from the NLT (New Living Translation) unless otherwise stated. Other scriptures used in this study include the HCSB (Holman Christian Standard Bible); NASB (New American Standard Bible); BSB (Berean Study Bible); CEV (Contemporary English Version); NIV (New International Version); Douay-Rheims Bible; ESV (English Standard Version); NET (New English Translation); Weymouth New Testament; BLB (BlueLetterBible.org); GNT (Good News Translation); and the KJV (King James Version).

Table of Contents

Introduction

The Book of Revelation has always been a book that fascinated and intimidated me. Not often do we hear much about it from the pulpit, and, when trying to study it on our own, we end up completely baffled by all the astounding sights John was privileged to see and by all the confusing symbolism. Add to that the fact that many events in this book appear to be out of chronological order and we see why the Book of Revelation has become a sadly neglected part of the Bible.

I'm no Bible scholar by any stretch of the imagination, but I've been a student and teacher of the Bible for more than 40 years and I've spent—and continue to spend—a lot of time reading the Word and looking over commentaries, concordances, and other study aids which help me better understand what I've been reading.

I'm also a wife, mother, and firm believer in Jesus Christ. I studied Women's Ministry at New Orleans Baptist Theological Seminary. You may also know me as the Bargainomics Lady. I spent more than a decade sharing money-saving tips on Birmingham's WBRC Fox 6 TV's morning show, "Good Day Alabama," and "News at Noon." I continue to do that on my website (Bargainomics.com) and Facebook page, as well as share a daily online Bible study in both places.

My husband Larry and I have read the Book of Revelation together and separately many times and, each time, learned and understood more about this book of prophecy. So many people make one attempt to read it and decide that the symbolism and chronology are impossible to grasp. But that's just not so.

Revelation can be broken down into understandable elements and segments, and I hope that's what I've accomplished here.

This study is divided into 141 short daily looks into the Revelation with each chapter spread over several days. The focal chapter is noted at the beginning of each day, so I hope you'll read and re-read each chapter as you begin each day's study. Some of you may want to read straight through the entire study. However you choose to read it, I hope it helps you become more comfortable with studying the Revelation and gives you more understanding of God's final message in the Bible.

Revelation 1

Day 1

This is a revelation from Jesus Christ, which God gave him to show his servants the events that must soon take place. He sent an angel to present this revelation to his servant John, who faithfully reported everything he saw. This is his report of the word of God and the testimony of Jesus Christ (Revelation 1:1-2).

We're diving into the Book of Revelation. Note that it's a single revelation, not plural as you often hear said: Revelations. The word translated as ***revelation*** comes from the ancient Greek word *apokalupsis*, meaning "apocalypse," or a revealing or unveiling.

This revelation was given to John the Apostle, not John the Baptist. If you look at Mark 6, you'll see that John the Baptist was beheaded long before John the Apostle was given this divine revelation. John the Baptist is quoted in some places in the Gospels (the books of Matthew, Mark, Luke, and John), but he wrote none of the New Testament. The Apostle John not only recorded ***this revelation from Jesus Christ,*** he also wrote the Gospel of John, as well as the books of First, Second, and Third John.

To understand Revelation, you need to be familiar with the rest of the Bible. Bible study is an important daily practice—not merely reading but using a good study Bible or reliable commentary to help you understand as you read. Psalm 49:20 speaks of *[m]an in his pomp, yet without understanding* (NASB). There is little benefit to reading the Bible unless we understand what we're reading. James 4:2 reminds us: *You do not have, because you do not ask* (BSB). As you begin this study, and as you read your Bible, pray and ask the Lord for understanding.

If you're a KJV person, consider reading a New King James Version (NKJV). As incentive, I highly recommend you compare the KJV and other translations of First Kings 16:11 and First Samuel 25:34 to see how drastically language has changed over the centuries.

Now back to Revelation. Notice this isn't John's revelation—it's *a revelation from Jesus Christ.* About what? *[T]he events that must soon take place.* It's been 2,000 years and these events still haven't taken place. Is the Bible in error? Never. The word translated *soon* is another ancient Greek phrase, *en tachei,* meaning "suddenly happening." It doesn't mean these things will take place soon after the Revelation has been given but that at whatever time they take place, they will begin suddenly. (*Tachei* refers to speed or rapidity, which is why its Greek root word is the basis for our word "tachometer.")

What's the purpose of the message of Revelation? *[T]o show his servants* the future. For many years, preachers and teachers steered clear of Revelation because of its confusing symbolism and its dire warning: *And I solemnly declare to everyone who hears the words of prophecy written in this book: If anyone adds anything to what is written here, God will add to that person the plagues described in this book* (Revelation 22:18). But the Revelation has been given and shouldn't be ignored.

So there's a bit of starter under our belts. I'm excited to share this study with you, and I hope you're looking forward to digging deeper.

4

Day 2

As we begin this look at the Book of Revelation, remember: (1) For the most part, John is describing things of the future, things he's never seen. Picture someone from 2,000 years ago trying to describe TVs and cell phones, trying to explain hearing voices and seeing pictures that appear seemingly right out of thin air. John's mission is not an easy one. (2) And John has a second difficult task: to describe things he is privileged to see in heaven.

The Apostle Paul notes one occasion when he was given a glimpse of heaven: *I was caught up to the third heaven fourteen years ago. Whether I was in my body or out of my body, I don't know—only God knows.... I was caught up to paradise and heard things so astounding that they cannot be expressed in words, things no human is allowed to tell* (2 Corinthians 12:2, 4).

The Book of Revelation certainly isn't light reading, but it's an invaluable study for every believer. It even opens with the offer of a special blessing: *The one who reads this is blessed, and those who hear the words of this prophecy and keep what is written in it are blessed, because the time is near!* (Revelation 1:3, HCSB).

Where was John when he received this *revelation from Jesus Christ*? John tells us: *I was exiled to the island of Patmos for preaching the word of God and for my testimony about Jesus. It was the Lord's Day* (Revelation 1:9b-10a).

John, now elderly, had been brought to this island prison *for preaching the word of God.* He'd been telling people *about Jesus.* And for that, the Romans took away his freedom. Or so they thought. But John knew the truth of Jesus' own words as he recorded them in John 8:36: *If the Son therefore shall make you free, ye shall be free indeed* (KJV). John's body may have been trapped on a tiny, isolated island, but his spirit was *free indeed.*

Please continue to re-read the day's focal chapter as you begin each day's study.

Day 3

This letter is from John to the seven churches in the province of Asia. I heard behind me a loud voice like a trumpet blast. It said, 'Write in a book everything you see, and send it to the seven churches in the cities of Ephesus, Smyrna, Pergamum, Thyatira, Sardis, Philadelphia, and Laodicea' (Revelation 1:4, 10b-11).

[T]he province of Asia. At the time John received this Revelation from Jesus Christ, Asia was part of the Roman Empire. John wasn't talking about the entire continent of Asia, but part of what is now the country of Turkey, and he was instructed to write down this message and share it with a select group of *seven churches in the cities of Ephesus, Smyrna, Pergamum, Thyatira, Sardis, Philadelphia, and Laodicea.*

Who is this *loud voice like a trumpet blast*? He has already identified himself in the previous verses. In verse 8, he says: *I am the Alpha and the Omega—the beginning and the end ... I am the one who is, who always was, and who is still to come—the Almighty One.* Only the Lord Jesus Christ holds this title, so it is Jesus himself speaking to John at this point in the Revelation. If you read a red-letter Bible, you'll see this passage and more in red, because Jesus is speaking.

When I saw him, I fell at his feet as if I were dead. But he laid his right hand on me and said, 'Don't be afraid! I am the First and the Last. I am the living one. I died, but look—I am alive forever and ever! And I hold the keys of death and the grave. Write down what you have seen—both the things that are now happening and the things that will happen' (Revelation 1:17-19). Jesus is not only speaking directly to John, but John is seeing him! Can you even imagine?

We're going to begin a look at the glorified Jesus tomorrow. But for now, let me ask: Do you want to see Jesus? A much younger John began his Gospel with: *In the beginning the Word already existed. The Word was with God, and the Word was God* (John 1:1). The Living Word inhabits every page of the Bible. Read it and you'll grow to know him better.

Day 4

John takes one look at the glorified Jesus and what happens? *When I saw him, I fell at his feet as if I were dead* (Revelation 1:17a). Jesus immediately reassured him: *Don't be afraid!* (Revelation 1:17b).

But it was hard not to be. Revelation 1:12-16 describes the scene that's taking place: *When I turned to see who was speaking to me, I saw seven gold lampstands. And standing in the middle of the lampstands was someone like the Son of Man. He was wearing a long robe with a gold sash across his chest. His head and his hair were white like wool, as white as snow. And his eyes were like flames of fire. His feet were like polished bronze refined in a furnace, and his voice thundered like mighty ocean waves. He held seven stars in his right hand, and a sharp two-edged sword came from his mouth. And his face was like the sun in all its brilliance.*

John sees *seven gold lampstands.* A lampstand serves one purpose: to hold a lamp. And a lamp serves one purpose: to bring light into a place that would otherwise be in darkness. Jesus said in John 9:5: *[W]hile I am here in the world, I am the light of the world.*

But look at Jesus' words from the Sermon on the Mount. He said of those who would believe in him: *You are the light of the world* (Matthew 5:14a). The Holy Spirit, Christ himself, indwells every true believer, making each one a *[l]ight ... in the darkness* (Psalm 112:4a).

And what is the church but a body of believers? *Light ... in the darkness.* Seven, being the number of perfection or completion in the Bible, points us to the Church, the body of Christ, as represented by the *seven gold lampstands.* The lampstand has no ability to produce light, but it can hold forth the light so that others see it.

Jesus never designated nor intended his body to be broken into factions of this and that denomination. He is the Head of the Church, regardless of what denominational name is on the sign outside.

But, as I said, the Church is made up of believers. If Jesus is your Lord and Savior, you are the Church. I am the Church. Are we shining forth his light? In this age of darkness, it's more important than ever to keep our lights shining.

Day 5

Yesterday we saw that *the lampstands* represented the Church. In the very midst of the Church we see *the Son of Man,* Jesus. Daniel also sees the glorified Christ in Daniel 7:13b-14: *I saw someone like a Son of Man coming with the clouds of heaven. He approached the Ancient One and was led into his presence. He was given authority, honor, and sovereignty over all the nations of the world, so that people of every race and nation and language would obey him. His rule is eternal—it will never end. His kingdom will never be destroyed.*

Yesterday's passage, Revelation 1:12-16, gives us some important details about the appearance of the glorified Lord. He is *wearing a long robe with a gold sash across his chest.* Here is a picture of Jesus as our High Priest. Part of the job of a priest in the temple was to tend the lamps, making sure they were clean and filled with oil. Jesus, as our Eternal High Priest, watches over his Church to encourage the Church and to inspect it. Remember: every true believer is part of the Church, the body of Christ.

His head and his hair were white like wool, as white as snow. White hair was a sign of old age and wisdom. Unlike the disregard for the elderly we see in American culture today, many cultures still have great respect for the aged. To see the Risen Savior with *hair ... white as snow* pointed to his wisdom and his eternality. Jesus Christ is *the one who always was, who is, and who is still to come* (Revelation 4:8b) and *his kingdom will never end!* (Luke 1:33b).

[H]is eyes were like flames of fire. The penetrating gaze of Jesus was as *flames of fire,* seeing into the very hearts of men and judging each one accordingly.

11

His feet were like polished bronze refined in a furnace. Bronze indicated strength and permanence. If you look in Exodus 27 at the description of the altar in the temple, you'll see that the entire altar was covered in bronze. Jesus Christ became our Living Sacrifice, placing himself on the altar of the cross as the One Perfect Sacrifice who would pay mankind's sin-debt for all time.

And the cost to me and you? ***Only believe*** (Mark 5:36, Luke 8:50b, HCSB). Do you?

Day 6

We're continuing our look at the glorified Jesus. *[His] voice thundered like mighty ocean waves. He held seven stars in his right hand, and a sharp two-edged sword came from his mouth* (Revelation 1:15b-16a).

He spoke with his powerful voice of authority and *held seven stars in his right hand.* What were these *seven stars*? The leaders of the seven churches (seven being the number of completion) with whom John was instructed to share this message: *Write in a book everything you see, and send it to the seven churches in the cities of Ephesus, Smyrna, Pergamum, Thyatira, Sardis, Philadelphia, and Laodicea* (Revelation 1:11).

If we look down to Revelation 1:20, we see the words of Jesus clearly explaining the stars and lampstands: *This is the meaning of the mystery of the seven stars you saw in my right hand and the seven gold lampstands: The seven stars are the angels of the seven churches, and the seven lampstands are the seven churches.* In some translations, the word *angels* is written as "messengers" or "ministers." Jesus upholds his godly messengers, whether human or angelic, and Jesus upholds his Church.

[A]nd a sharp two-edged sword came from His mouth." You may be thinking you've read a similar passage in Hebrews: *"For the Word of God is alive and powerful. It is sharper than the sharpest two-edged sword* (Hebrews 4:12a). However, there's a difference in the two words translated as *two-edged sword* in the Revelation and Hebrews passages.

In the Hebrews passage, *two-edged sword* is translated from the Greek word *machairan* while in Revelation the *two-edged sword* is a translation of the word *rhomphaia*. In the first word, we see more of a double-edged knife, something used in up-close warfare, **cutting between soul and spirit, between joint and marrow** (Hebrews 4:12b). The sword in Revelation is a broad, long sword, far-reaching and capable of horrific destruction.

Both swords represent **the Word of God**, which **exposes our innermost thoughts and desires.** Names on church rolls won't fool Jesus when he calls out his Church. Only those who have truly received him as Lord and Savior are part of the One True Church. And only those have the believer's single offensive weapon, **the sword of the Spirit, which is the Word of God** (Ephesians 6:17).

So did John actually see a sword coming out of the mouth of Jesus? I don't think so. What I am sure of is that the **Word of God** came from him and should also come from us as his children. No earthly weapon can help us fight our battles (see Ephesians 6:12), but the **Word of God** will always bring defeat to the enemy. Know it and use it.

Day 7

And standing in the middle of the lampstands was someone like the Son of Man ... And his face was like the sun in all its brilliance (Revelation 1:13a, 16b).

So many Bible passages come to mind when I read this description of the glorified Jesus. Think about the shepherds to whom Jesus' birth was announced: ***Suddenly, an angel of the Lord appeared among them, and the radiance of the Lord's glory surrounded them*** (Luke 2:9a). Because that angel (and the ***vast host*** of angels who appeared soon after the first angel—see Luke 2:13), had been in the presence of God, he shone with ***the radiance of the Lord's glory***.

Hebrews 1:3a declares: ***The Son radiates God's own glory.*** Psalm 50:2b says: ***God shines in glorious radiance.*** And in the Old Testament, Moses' ***face had become radiant because he had spoken to the Lord*** (Exodus 34:29b). A mere glimpse of his Creator set Moses' face aglow with the radiance of God.

Even before Jesus' resurrection and ascension, John, along with Peter and James, were allowed to see his glory on the Mount of Transfiguration: ***Jesus' appearance was transformed so that his face shone like the sun, and his clothes became as white as light*** (Matthew 17:2b).

The light of the Savior reveals everything. Nothing is hidden from him. Our darkest secrets are exposed. Anything false within us is laid bare. Understanding this truth should create in each of us a tremendous sense of urgency to live for Christ and to tell others about him.

Jesus instructed John to *[w]rite down what you have seen—both the things that are now happening and the things that will happen* (Revelation 1:19). This sentence gives us the three-part breakdown of the Revelation: (1) Chapter 1: *what you have seen*; (2) Chapters 2-3: *the things that are now happening*; and (3) Chapters 4-22: *the things that will happen.*

Chapters 2 and 3 contain the letters to the seven churches, all of which were *in the province of Asia* (Revelation 1:4). As we've already seen, *Asia* didn't refer to the entire continent of Asia, but to part of what is now the country of Turkey. We'll begin our look at the churches tomorrow. I hope you'll go ahead and read Chapters 2 and 3.

Revelation 2

Day 8

The second chapter of the Revelation opens with these instructions from the Lord Jesus Christ to the Apostle John: ***Write this letter to the angel of the church of Ephesus*** (Revelation 2:1a).

As mentioned previously, the word translated ***angel*** in the NLT and many translations is also translated as "messenger" or "minister" in others. While an angel of the Lord certainly watches over his Church, this message was directed to the leader or pastor of the church at Ephesus, who would then share the letter with the entire congregation.

Remember, the epistles, such as the book of Romans, are simply letters written to specific churches, with Romans being the Apostle Paul's letter to the church in Rome and Ephesians being his letter to the church in Ephesus.

Ephesus was a prominent city, being the capital of the province of Asia, as well as the location of the temple of the Roman goddess Diana, who was known to the Greeks as Artemis. If you read Acts 19, you'll see that Paul spent at least two years teaching in Ephesus, and many people put their faith in Jesus Christ during that time. This infuriated the silversmith tradesmen, because a huge part of their income came from making household-sized images of Diana.

Like so many pagan religions, the worship of Diana involved sexual immorality, with temple prostitutes a part of the rites of this belief. Think about having been part of such a perverted form of worship, then learning about Jesus, repenting, and walking away from all that. The Christians of Ephesus had come out of an empty and immoral lifestyle which continued to be a thriving part of the Ephesian culture.

We like to blame the internet and television and all sorts of modern-day media for how difficult it is to live a moral lifestyle today. "There's just so much temptation out there!" News flash: that's not news. Temptation has been around since the Garden of Eden.

It's up to every Christian to be 100 percent genuine in their commitment to Christ. God's Word reminds us now just as it did then: *The temptations in your life are no different from what others experience. And God is faithful. He will not allow the temptation to be more than you can stand. When you are tempted, he will show you a way out so that you can endure* (1 Corinthians 10:13).

Day 9

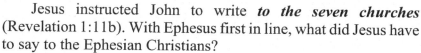

Jesus instructed John to write *to the seven churches* (Revelation 1:11b). With Ephesus first in line, what did Jesus have to say to the Ephesian Christians?

I know all the things you do. I have seen your hard work and your patient endurance. I know you don't tolerate evil people. You have examined the claims of those who say they are apostles but are not. You have discovered they are liars. You have patiently suffered for me without quitting (Revelation 2:2-3).

First, we see a statement Jesus says to every believer: *I know all the things you do.* The Holy Spirit, Jesus himself, indwells every true believer, and he indeed knows everything about us.

Jesus then commended the Ephesian believers for their *hard work and ... patient endurance.* The church at Ephesus was working hard for the Kingdom of God, and they didn't put up with false *apostles* who tried to infiltrate their congregation and lead them away from the truth.

Despite all that, though, Jesus goes on to say: *But I have this complaint against you. You don't love me or each other as you did at first!* (Revelation 2:4). On the surface, everything at the First Church of Ephesus looked great. But when Jesus took a peek below their carefully plastered façade, he saw people who went through all the right motions but without their initial love.

Newlyweds may be absolutely giddy about their new life and love together, but after a while that giddiness settles down. If that marriage is healthy, though, the love continues to grow and mature. It may not be as flamboyant as it was in the beginning, but the depth of that love assuredly increases.

Likewise, a Christian's love for the Lord and for his fellow believers should continue to grow. When that love is diminishing rather than growing, a Christian is simply going through the motions rather than seriously pursuing a deeper walk with the Savior. *God is love* (1 John 4:8 and 16), and no one can grow closer to him without loving him more and loving others more too.

How long have you been a believer? Can you honestly say you love Jesus Christ more today than you did the day you committed your heart and life to him? If you do, how do you show it in your prayer life? Bible study? Church attendance? Financial giving? Treatment of others?

The Lord has more to say to the Ephesians and more to say to us through this letter. We'll get back at it tomorrow.

Day 10

We're looking at Jesus' letter to the church in Ephesus, the first of the seven letters he instructed John to write. He commended them for the positive things they were doing, then added: ***But I have this complaint against you. You don't love me or each other as you did at first!*** (Revelation 2:4). He saw this bunch of believers exemplifying servanthood but without the love for him or others that they'd had at the beginning of their commitment to him.

This church was busy, doing good, steering clear of all the evil that surrounded them in their goddess-worshiping city, and making sure no false teachers or ***apostles*** sneaked into their congregation. But even with all that, Jesus said to them: ***Look how far you have fallen!*** (Revelation 2:5a).

A marriage with love that isn't nurtured can become more of an institution than a commitment. This is what Jesus was saying to the church in Ephesus. They still met regularly; they still did good deeds; they avoided all wrongdoing; but their love had dwindled rather than grown. In a marriage, a couple can get so busy going through day-to-day routines that they forget to consciously seek to grow in love for each other. This is what had happened in the church of Ephesus.

So Jesus warned them: ***Turn back to me and do the works you did at first*** (Revelation 2:5b).

Turn back to me. The church that was doing everything right needed to repent. Why? Because of what they weren't doing. Jesus quoted Deuteronomy 6:5 to the Pharisees, those pious worshipers who kept every letter of the Mosaic Law: ***'You must***

21

love the Lord your God with all your heart, all your soul, and all your mind.' This is the first and greatest commandment (Matthew 22:37-38).

To break a commandment of God is to sin. And the Ephesian church was in sin because of their diminishing love for Christ and, subsequently, for others, which is why Jesus went on to say: *If you don't repent, I will come and remove your lampstand from its place among the churches* (Revelation 2:5c).

Jesus didn't and doesn't want a band of robots going through the motions of the Christian lifestyle. After all, he doesn't need us, period. He does, however, love us, and that alone is beyond comprehension when we look at our own lives and the priorities we value more than him.

How would Jesus *come and remove* the *lampstand*, representing the church at Ephesus, *from its place among the churches*? The church might keep the doors open and continue to do business as usual, but the favor of God would no longer be on that congregation.

The same is true of an individual Christian's life. If a person wants the approval of God and the favor of God, then he or she must obey *the greatest commandment* and *love the Lord your God with all your heart, all your soul, and all your mind.*

Day 11

Before we wrap up our look at the church in Ephesus, I want to touch on two different lines of thinking about what is represented by the seven churches to whom Jesus instructed John to write.

Some Bible scholars believe each church represents a church age or time period. Most don't agree with that viewpoint, including John MacArthur, who says of the letters to the seven churches: "When Christ speaks to those churches, he is speaking to all the churches of all time.... There is tremendous prophetic importance in those churches because their messages represent the total message to the total church."

In other words, we need to listen up because all these messages are for the church of today just as they were for the church of John's day, and every time period between then and now. And let me reiterate that the True Church is not a denomination but is composed of all true believers worldwide.

Two important things we need to note here and consider over the next few days:

(1) Before Jesus dictates each of the seven letters to the churches, he instructs John: *Write this letter to the angel of the church in ...* (Revelation 2:1, 8, 12, 18; 3:1, 7, 14). An angel of God assuredly watches over the Church, but the letter was to be read aloud to the entire congregation, making it most likely that these letters were addressed to the human messenger, as in the pastor of each congregation.

(2) Jesus closes his message to the Ephesian church as well as the other six churches with these words: *Anyone with ears to*

hear must listen to the Spirit and understand what he is saying to the churches (Revelation 2:7a, 11a, 17a, 29; 3:6, 13, 22). You can sit in church every Sunday and ***hear*** the sermon, but unless you also ***understand***, it becomes easy to leave church having gotten nothing out of the service and having put nothing into it. Just as with reading the Bible, God doesn't want us to merely read the words; he wants us to ***understand*** and apply them.

Have you ever sat in church and thought, "I wish So-and-So were here because this message is sure for her!" I'll put my hand up and admit I've done that. Reminds me of a humorous yet serious quote by the great theologian Henry Ward Beecher: "The churches of the land are sprinkled all over with bald-headed old sinners whose hair has been worn off by the constant friction of countless sermons that have been aimed at them and glanced off and hit the man in the pew behind."

May all us "bald-headed sinners" become "the man in the pew behind."

Day 12

After instructing John to *[w]rite this letter*, Jesus opened each letter with a distinct statement. In the case of the church of Ephesus, Jesus said: ***This is the message from the one who holds the seven stars in his right hand, the one who walks among the seven gold lampstands*** (Revelation 2:1b).

Jesus told John to write to the churches. How was he to get those messages to the churches? After all, he was exiled on an island. There are a couple reasonable explanations:

(1) Boats came and went from the island, bringing supplies and other prisoners. John could have sent the messages by boat. Possible, yes, but my vote is for the second possibility.

(2) Historical records indicate John was released from prison shortly after he recorded Jesus' Revelation message. Ephesus was a coastal city and only a short boat trip from Patmos. The other six churches were all within a reasonable distance from Ephesus, so John may have personally delivered the message to all seven churches.

According to all available information, John appears to be the only apostle who lived to a very old age and apparently died of natural causes. Being the last of the original 12 disciples who walked and talked with Jesus, we can only imagine the excitement of having John walk into the church at Ephesus or any of the other six churches. Too, this final message of Jesus Christ would be held in high regard and copies of the entire Revelation made and distributed to not only the seven churches but to all the churches.

So even though seven specific churches were designated as recipients and the specific goings-on—both good and bad—

within those churches are addressed, the message is for all churches in all ages, including today. Seven, signifying completion, encompasses the entire true Church, which may be why Jesus chose to begin the first of his letters, the one to Ephesus, identifying himself as the one with the ***seven stars*** and ***seven gold lampstands***. I pray each person reading this is part of the One True Church.

Day 13

Jesus closed his message to the Ephesian church as well as the other six churches with these words: ***Anyone with ears to hear must listen to the Spirit and understand what he is saying to the churches*** (Revelation 2:7a, 11a, 17a, 29; 3:6, 13, 22). Just as he followed *[w]rite this letter to the angel of the church in ...* (Revelation 2:1, 8, 12, 18; 3:1, 7, 14) each location with a distinct statement, Jesus concluded the Ephesian letter and the other six letters with distinct statements.

To Ephesus, he said: ***To everyone who is victorious I will give fruit from the tree of life in the paradise of God*** (Revelation 2:7b).

What did Jesus want the church at Ephesus to be ***victorious*** over? Their lack of love for him and others. Love doesn't rekindle itself. We have to consciously seek to rebuild it.

When a marriage vow is broken, it takes a heap of work to keep that marriage together and reconnect the trust and love that should be there. Easy? No. But I know couples who've been through major storms and refused to give up on each other. Let me add right here that I am totally aware that it takes two willing parties to save a marriage.

And speaking of marriage, every believer is part of the Bride of Christ. No matter how unfaithful you or I have been to our Bridegroom, he still loves us. He'll still forgive us. He won't give up on us. He wants our love for him to grow and mature, just as he wanted to see the church at Ephesus continue to not only do all the right things, but to get back to doing them in love. And he wanted to see that love turn from declining to increasing.

I will give fruit from the tree of life in the paradise of God. Where was *the tree of life*? Eden, man's original *paradise*. But *the paradise of God*? This was the dwelling place of our Creator. What did Jesus say to the repentant thief on the cross? *[T]oday you will be with me in paradise* (Luke 23:43b).

This is such a significant promise, and it wasn't merely for the Ephesian Christians who heeded Jesus' words. It's also for every believer today who will listen and obey. Jesus' promise is for here and the hereafter.

We can eat of the *fruit from the tree of life* not only in *the paradise of God*, but we can eat of the spiritual *fruit from the tree of life* right now if we're putting God first (see Matthew 6:33). Meaning what exactly? When we're fully committed to Jesus Christ, we miss out on many of the effects of the curse (see Genesis 3).

Will our lives be worry-free? No. The Bible makes it clear we live in a fallen world where bad things happen to good people. But I can promise you this: when you put God first, you position yourself for blessings. Materially? Maybe. Spiritually? Most definitely. And when you do reach *the paradise of God*, you'll be astounded to learn all the negative things that were kept from your life because of your faithfulness.

Day 14

Jesus' first letter was to the church in Ephesus. His second letter begins: *To the angel of the church in Smyrna write ...* (Revelation 2:8a).

What sort of city was Smyrna? It was a riverfront community with a burgeoning import/export trade via its harbor, which made it a very wealthy city. It also brought in people from a variety of places and beliefs. Smryna's own citizens traveled and experienced many other cultures and religions. These cults were introduced into Smyrna and received with open arms, with temples dedicated to the worship of Apollo, Cybele, and Zeus, among many others.

But all these worship centers fizzled into the background when in 196 BC Smyrna built the first temple to "Dea Roma"—*dea* being the female form of the word god, signifying a goddess, and *Roma* meaning Rome. The Goddess of Rome became Smyrna's trendiest deity and her temple the most popular place to worship.

Bear in mind the message of Revelation wasn't written until AD and most Bible scholars date it somewhere between the years AD 70 and 96. The later date seems more feasible because historical records point to Domitian as the emperor who sentenced John to exile on Patmos, and Domitian was emperor from AD 81 to 96.

By the time of the Revelation, the worship of the Goddess of Rome had changed to the worship of the Roman Emperor himself. Domitian was particularly cruel to Christians, considering himself a god and demanding the title of "dominus et deus," meaning "lord and god." Domitian's rule didn't make it easy for Christians in Smyrna, and that came as no surprise to Jesus. After all, he'd told his disciples: *Here on earth you will have many trials and sorrows* (John 16:33b). However, he also said: *But take heart, because I have overcome the world* (John 16:33c).

Good News for Smyrna and Good News for us today.

Day 15

In Jesus' letter to the church of Smyrna, he said: *These are the words of the First and the Last, who died and returned to life* (Revelation 2:8b). How important are those words to the Christians of Smyrna in light of his message to these believers?

I know your affliction and your poverty—though you are rich! And I am aware of the slander of those who falsely claim to be Jews, but are in fact a synagogue of Satan. Do not fear what you are about to suffer. Look, the devil is about to throw some of you into prison to test you, and you will suffer tribulation for ten days. Be faithful even unto death, and I will give you the crown of life (Revelation 2:9-10).

It's going to take a while to pick all this apart, so I hope you'll bear with me, but first we see Jesus telling them: *I know your affliction and your poverty....* Smyrna was a wealthy city, yet the Christians lived in extreme poverty, the poorest of the poor. Why? People didn't want to hire Christians. People didn't want anything to do with Christians. To profess Jesus as Lord was to be shunned in society, and that included ways to make a living.

[T]hough you are rich! The strong faith it took to stand for Jesus Christ in the face of such discrimination and cruelty didn't go unnoticed. Nor would it go unrewarded. John Trapp, a 15th century theologian, referred to Smyrna as "the poorest but purest of the seven." Contrary to what this world teaches, what we have here on Earth matters little. What's important is to *store your treasure in heaven* (Matthew 6:20a). That is exactly what the Smyrna Christians were doing.

31

And I am aware of the slander of those who falsely claim to be Jews, but are in fact a synagogue of Satan. Smyrna included a large Jewish community, but those Jews were vehement opponents of anyone who professed to be a follower of Jesus. Paul had dealt with their kind many times, his life often threatened by Jews who refused to believe in Jesus as the Messiah. And the cold, unyielding hearts of these Jews in Smyrna prompted Jesus to call them what they'd become: *a synagogue of Satan.*

We may not experience persecution like the believers of Smyrna, but we definitely live in frightening times. Yet the Church still stands, and Jesus promises *all the powers of hell will not conquer it* (Matthew 16:18b). So stand firm, believers! God is on our side.

Day 16

Jesus gave this specific word to the church at Smryna: *These are the words of the First and the Last, who died and returned to life* (Revelation 2:8b). Yesterday I said this statement was important for the Christians of Smyrna. Why?

They were under tremendous persecution. If the latter timeline for the writing of the Revelation is correct—and I personally believe it is—then Domitian would have been the ruling emperor (81-96 AD). He was the ruler who demanded the title of "dominus et deus," meaning "lord and god." Like many religions today, tacking on one more "god" to worship wasn't a problem for many of the people in Smyrna, but for the Christians, it was completely unacceptable, and that meant facing the wrath of Domitian.

One of Domitian's favorite forms of torture was boiling people alive in oil, and his favorite targets were Christians. No wonder Jesus began his letter by identifying himself as *the First and the Last, who died and returned to life.* The faithful saints of God at Smyrna suffered horribly, but they did so knowing Christ's promise as Paul announced to King Agrippa: *the Messiah would suffer and be the first to rise from the dead* (Acts 26:23a).

Many of the Smyrna believers lost their lives under Domitian's reign of terror, but they did so fully confident that Jesus, *the first to rise from the dead*, would *raise them up* (Jesus speaking, John 6:44b) into his eternal kingdom, just as he promised. Look again at Jesus' message to the church at Smyrna: *Look, the devil is about to throw some of you into prison to test you.... Be faithful even unto death, and I will give you the crown of life* (Revelation 2:10).

Remember again, every one of these letters is for the entire True Church. Christians are outcasts in many countries around the world today. They suffer untold horrors while we in America, for the most part, sit back and decide whether we want to take an hour or so out of our day for "church" or, instead, make a day of it at the lake or flea market or golf course.

The church in Smyrna is the only one of the seven churches that got a clean bill of health. Suffering changes us. It changes our focus. The person battling cancer isn't concerned about a new car or house or trip to Hawaii. And if that person knows the end is near, their focus is one of two places: faith or fear. They're either ready to meet their Maker or terrified of what comes next.

The people of Smyrna met their suffering with faith. None of us will get out this world alive, unless we're here when the Rapture takes place. Even if we are privileged to peacefully leave this world in our sleep, none of us will get to that point without enduring some form of suffering. I pray each of us will allow whatever hardships come our way to increase our faith and love for the Lord, because *perfect love expels all fear* (1 John 4:18b), and *God is love* (1 John 4:16b).

Day 17

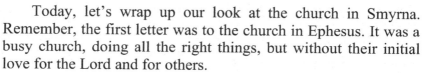

Today, let's wrap up our look at the church in Smyrna. Remember, the first letter was to the church in Ephesus. It was a busy church, doing all the right things, but without their initial love for the Lord and for others.

The church of Smyrna was faithfully serving the Lord in spite of tremendous persecution. Is there persecution in the Church today? In many countries, setting foot in a church is putting your life at risk. In America, look at the recent shootings that have occurred in churches.

According to a study done by the Center for Homicide Research, there were 139 shootings on church property in the U.S. between 1980 and 2005, resulting in the deaths of 185 people. And bear in mind, these murders were long before the more recent shootings like the ones at Emanuel AME in Charleston, South Carolina, which took the lives of nine people and First Baptist Church in Southerland Springs, Texas, where 26 people died. Christians have been and still are objects of hatred to many.

As with each of the seven letters, the Lord closed with: ***Anyone with ears to hear must listen to the Spirit and understand what he is saying to the churches*** (Revelation 2:11a). This is followed by Jesus' specific statement for the believers of Smyrna: ***Whoever is victorious will not be harmed by the second death*** (Revelation 2:11b).

What is this ***second death***? The Revelation leaves no doubt of its meaning: ***The lake of fire is the second death*** (Revelation 20:14b). And who should fear the ***second death***? ***[C]owards, unbelievers, the corrupt, murderers, the immoral, those who*** *practice witchcraft, idol worshipers, and all liars—their fate is in the fiery lake of burning sulfur. This is the second death* (Revelation 21:8).

Without making today's study too long, I can't expound on this particular list, but suffice it to say that everything listed here, along with the word *unbelievers*, describes lifestyles that in no way reflect faith in Jesus Christ. And as Peter states emphatically in Acts 4:12: *There is salvation in no one else! God has given no other name under heaven by which we must be saved.* The way to heaven is through a total commitment to the Lord Jesus Christ. There is no other way.

And for those who've made that commitment? The Book of Revelation has a message of assurance: *[T]he second death holds no power* (Revelation 20:6b), and as we've seen in the Lord's message to Smyrna: *Whoever is victorious will not be harmed by the second death* (Revelation 2:11b).

The Bible leaves no doubt that Jesus truly died for all: *He died for everyone* (2 Corinthians 5:15a), but not all accept his free gift of salvation. Jesus plainly states the final destination of those who don't: *Away with you, you cursed ones, into the eternal fire prepared for the devil and his demons* (Matthew 25:41b).

It is not, and never has been, God's will for a person to spend eternity in hell. Hell wasn't created for humankind but *for the devil and his demons.* There is no fence to straddle. It's Jesus or Satan, and each person must choose. Choose Jesus, and you've chosen eternity in heaven; reject him, and you've chosen eternal damnation. We need to be busy explaining this.

Day 18

Jesus' letters to the churches in Ephesus and Smyrna have been examined, and we have five more to cover, with the church at Pergamum coming up next.

To review, Ephesus was a busy church, but without the initial love for the Lord and for others that had been and should be the motivation behind every ministry. Smyrna is the only one of the seven churches given a clean bill of health. This church was under great persecution but was standing firm.

What about Pergamum? Jesus opened his address to the church in Pergamum with a stern reminder: ***This is the message from the one with the sharp two-edged sword*** (Revelation 2:12b). The word translated ***sword*** is again the word *rhomphaia*, a broad, long sword, far-reaching and capable of horrific destruction.

Jesus' message continues: ***I know that you live in the city where Satan has his throne, yet you have remained loyal to me. You refused to deny me even when Antipas, my faithful witness, was martyred among you there in Satan's city. But I have a few complaints against you. You tolerate some among you whose teaching is like that of Balaam, who showed Balak how to trip up the people of Israel. He taught them to sin by eating food offered to idols and by committing sexual sin*** (Revelation 2:13-15).

The Christians of Pergamum were surrounded by people who worshiped false gods, religions which, in many instances, included making use of shrine prostitutes as part of their practices. Roman culture in general was "if it feels good, do it." Christians were considered more than peculiar because they didn't follow this same self-indulgent philosophy.

With all that went on around them, the majority of those within the church at Pergamum had **remained loyal**, including a believer named Antipas, who was killed because of his faithful witness. But that same church also allowed people to stay in their congregation, fully aware that they were participating in the cultic worship of **eating food offered to idols and ... committing sexual sin.**

Eating food offered to idols may not sound like a big deal until you realize that these people weren't simply buying leftover ceremonial meat in the marketplace. They were attending the functions of these pagan places of worship and taking part in the ceremonies, which included not only eating the food but also **committing sexual sin.**

Pergamum had become a social club church. Even though many were sincere in their faith and walk with the Lord, others were using the church as a gathering place where they could simply see and be seen. And the leaders were doing nothing to stop this. How did Pergamum begin its downhill slide? Compromise. And Jesus warned He would not tolerate it: **Repent of your sin, or I will come to you suddenly and fight against them with the sword of my mouth** (Revelation 2:16).

In other words, clean up your church, or I will come and do it for you. He has the same message for any disobedient individual who is part of the True Church. God won't spank the devil's children, but he'll flat-out tan the hide of one of his own who refuses to repent and obey him. Stay on the right track. The Father never likes taking a child to the woodshed, but he loves each of us too much to let us continue wrongdoing.

Day 19

As we looked at yesterday, Jesus' third letter was a message to the church in Pergamum. Even though many were sincere in their faith, others were using the church as a social gathering place, and the leaders were tolerating this.

Some believers in Pergamum were not only attending church services, but also participating in the disgusting religious practices of some of the surrounding pagan temples. Compromise was killing the witness of the church, which is why Jesus concluded His letter with: ***Repent of your sin, or I will come to you suddenly and fight against them with the sword of my mouth*** (Revelation 2:16).

Note the exact wording of Jesus' warning: ***I will come to YOU suddenly and fight against THEM....*** Jesus' displeasure wasn't with the entire church. After all, a church is simply a body of believers, and some, not all, of Pergamum's believers had become filthy with sin. Jesus said he would ***come ... suddenly***, or unexpectedly. But he was specifically coming to deal with ***them***. Who's ***them***? The churchgoers who were also joining in pagan practices. These believers were living like hell itself outside the church and then coming into church expecting the Lord to bless them for simply showing up.

But that's not the only ***them*** I believe the Lord was addressing. He was also speaking of those who were in positions of authority within the church who were knowingly allowing these embarrassments to the name of Christ to continue unchecked.

It isn't every believer's job to point out the faults or sins of other believers. Even when a church member is absolutely certain of a serious problem within the church, there's an appropriate way to handle it. The church member should take their concern to the pastor or another person in authority within the congregation. That person should not share that information with anyone else within the congregation, and certainly not outside it. Above all, that person should pray for the involved party or parties to repent.

When any Christian cares more about how they look to other people than how they look to Christ, that Christian is compromising. And compromising is sin. We must keep our focus where it matters and look to and live for Jesus.

Day 20

Jesus ended his message to the church at Pergamum with these words: *Anyone with ears to hear must listen to the Spirit and understand what he is saying to the churches. To everyone who is victorious I will give some of the manna that has been hidden away in heaven. And I will give to each one a white stone, and on the stone will be engraved a new name that no one understands except the one who receives it* (Revelation 2:17).

Anyone with ears should heed the message and warning to the church at Pergamum. Remember, it's not just for the people of that church or that time period.

To everyone who is victorious I will give some of the manna that has been hidden away in heaven. The Bread of Life promises heaven *[t]o everyone who is victorious.* The sheep and the goats will be sorted—and until that time, only the Lord will know for certain which is which. The goats—those who are merely playing at being Christian—will not leave this life in victory. But the sheep—those who are truly born again through faith in Jesus Christ—will be *victorious.*

It is those born-again believers who will be given *a white stone, and on the stone will be engraved a new name that no one understands except the one who receives it.* What's the significance of *a white stone*? In John's day, public games or competitions were hugely popular. The champion in such a contest would be rewarded with a white stone engraved with that person's own name. Ownership of that stone meant the recipient never had to pay a dime for anything. He had free admission anywhere he wanted to go; free food wherever he wanted to eat; free everything.

For the believer, the ***white stone*** represents Christ's promise to eternally welcome and care for that member of the family of God. And the ***new name***? I don't know exactly what that means, but I do know there won't be two people with the same name in heaven. No one's going to confuse John the Apostle with John the Baptist. Everyone will have a ***new name***, and the Lord himself will give that ***new name*** to each believer.

How will it be ***a name that no one understands except the one who receives it***? I believe God's love for each believer is intimate beyond our comprehension. He will give each of us a name based on something so specific and personal to our own relationship with him that only the individual child of God and the Father himself will know and understand why that name was chosen.

This ***white stone*** and ***new name*** was Jesus' promise to the faithful in Pergamum, and it's his promise to true believers today.

And you will be given a new name by the Lord's own mouth (Isaiah 62:2b).

Day 21

So far, we've looked at Jesus' letters to the churches of Ephesus, Smyrna, and Pergamum. Now we come to Thyatira. Jesus included a specific statement in both the opening and closing of each of the seven letters. To the church at Thyatira, he identified himself as *the Son of God, whose eyes are like flames of fire, whose feet are like polished bronze* (Revelation 2:18b).

This identification is significant for the Thyatirans because of what Jesus is going to say to them. First, he declared His deity: *the Son of God*. He's not *a* god. He's *the* God. The One and Only.

Next, Jesus said his *eyes are like flames of fire*. This description speaks of his penetrating gaze of judgment. Nothing is hidden from him. Everything good and evil is laid bare before him.

And then he says his *feet are like polished bronze*. Here we see purity, strength, and permanence. As Jesus identified himself to John at the beginning of the Revelation, Jesus is *the Alpha and the Omega—the beginning and the end ... the one who is, who always was, and who is still to come—the Almighty One* (Revelation 1:8). He's always been and always will be.

Jesus then commended some of the people in the church at Thyatira: *I know all the things you do. I have seen your love, your faith, your service, and your patient endurance. And I can see your constant improvement in all these things* (Revelation 2:19). Not only did the church at Thyatira have *love, ... faith, ... service, and ... patient endurance*, they were growing in these positive attributes. However, there was still a big, ugly problem.

43

But I have this complaint against you. You are permitting that woman—that Jezebel who calls herself a prophet—to lead my servants astray. She teaches them to commit sexual sin and to eat food offered to idols (Revelation 2:20).

Right in the middle of the church was a woman who had been accepted as a prophetess, someone to be looked up to and respected, and this woman was leading church members into all the things pagan religions were promoting. Unlike Pergamum who had members dabbling in both places, this woman was apparently teaching inside the church, and some of the congregation were joining in with her immoral beliefs and behavior.

How can such a thing be allowed inside a church not merely professing to serve Jesus, but growing in *love, … faith, … service, and … patient endurance*? Where there are sheep, there are wolves. As unbelievable as it may seem, I recently read an article about a supposedly Christian church in Virginia that offers nude worship.

The Lord will not allow his people to continue in sin. Not me. Not you. Not anyone who belongs to his family. Tomorrow we'll see how he will deal with Thyatira.

Day 22

Nahum 1:3a reminds us: *The Lord is powerful, yet patient* (CEV). The Lord had given the false prophetess within the church at Thyatira *time to repent,* but she had continued doing evil and was pulling others along with her. The Lord said he'd seen and had enough. She and those who'd taken up with her were about to *suffer greatly unless they repent and turn away from her evil deeds.*

How would this so-called *Jezebel* suffer? *I will strike her children dead. Then all the churches will know that I am the one who searches out the thoughts and intentions of every person. And I will give to each of you whatever you deserve* (Revelation 2:23).

Who were this false prophetess' *children*? Those who followed her teaching. And *unless they* [chose to] *repent and turn away from her evil deeds*, they and the prophetess herself would *suffer greatly*, possibly in physical death, but also in *the second death*. As we looked at a while back: *This lake of fire is the second death. And anyone whose name was not found recorded in the Book of Life was thrown into the lake of fire* (Revelation 20:14b-15).

Can a truly born-again believer be drawn into such evil? If you recall the supposedly Christian church that I mentioned yesterday offering nude worship, you see an entire church drawn into evil. And whether I think all those people are hell-bound or not, I'm not their judge. God is. He alone knows who's stumbled off the right pathway and who's never been on it in the first place.

45

A pastor I'll call Wally began a relationship with a married woman at his church. This woman actually wrote sermons for him. He eventually left his wife and family and the woman left hers with plans to begin their own ministry. When I tried to talk to Wally, he told me, "I know this sounds crazy, but I know this is God's will."

Nope, it was never God's will. Wally lost everything. This woman lost everything. No "ministry" transpired and the pair grew to loathe each other. After a long time, Wally repented and was forgiven by a loving wife and family. More importantly, he was forgiven by God.

Wally told me about his experience. He said, "The Holy Spirit put up red flag after red flag in my spirit when that woman started sending me little notes and dropping by my office. I ignored every one of them."

Nobody gets away with sin. As Jesus plainly warned the Thyatirans, *I am the one who searches out the thoughts and intentions of every person. And I will give to each of you whatever you deserve.*

I don't know about you, but when I think of how often I have failed him in the past and still continue to fail him, the thoughts of getting what I deserve is terrifying. All the more reason to stay 'fessed up, prayed up, and busy for the Kingdom. Is that what you're doing?

Day 23

The Lord had given the false prophetess within the church at Thyatira *time to repent* (Revelation 2:21a), but she had continued doing evil and pulling others along with her. And the Lord said enough was enough. She and those who'd taken up with her were about to *suffer greatly unless they repent and turn away from her evil deeds* (Revelation 2:22b).

Look closely at what else Jesus had to say to the church at Thyatira. He wasn't going to inflict punishment on the whole congregation: *But I also have a message for the rest of you in Thyatira who have not followed this false teaching ('deeper truths,' as they call them—depths of Satan, actually). I will ask nothing more of you except that you hold tightly to what you have until I come* (Revelation 2:24-25).

The Lord had already told the rest of the Thyatiran congregation: *I know all the things you do. I have seen your love, your faith, your service, and your patient endurance. And I can see your constant improvement in all these things* (Revelation 2:19).

The Lord always knows everything going on everywhere, and apparently the majority of the believers at Thyatira were sticking to the truth and not only living by it but growing in it, which is why Jesus' word to them was to simply keep on doing what they were doing.

To all who are victorious, who obey me to the very end, To them I will give authority over all the nations. They will rule the nations with an iron rod and smash them like clay pots. They will have the same authority I received from my Father, and I will also give them the morning star! (Revelation 2:26-28).

Jesus promises victory to all ***who obey ... to the very end.*** I remember witnessing to my neighbor who had grown up in a church where there was enormous emphasis on outward emotion. All her siblings had been on fire for the Lord one minute and living like the devil the next. Over and over and over. When I tried to talk to her about my faith, she stopped me in my tracks, saying, "Don't tell me. Show me." In other words, she let me know she was watching me and expected to see a consistent lifestyle of faith. It was at least 20 years before I saw her and her husband surrender to the Lordship of Jesus, but when they did, they were sold-out believers.

In verses 27-28 above, Jesus is quoting from Psalm 2:8-9. No doubt the sinful behavior of the prophetess and her followers was terribly distressing to the faithful at Thyatira. But the Lord sent them a message of hope and comfort: they would one day rule and reign with him, Christ, the Morning Star.

Jesus closes his message to the church at Thyatira with: ***Anyone with ears to hear must listen to the Spirit and understand what he is saying to the churches.*** Church, are you listening?

Revelation 3

Day 24

We've seen the letters to the churches at Ephesus, Smyrna, Pergamum, and Thyatira. Now we come to Sardis. As in every letter, the Lord began by instructing John to *[w]rite this letter to the angel* [or messenger or pastor] *of the church* (Revelation 3:1a), in this case, *in Sardis*. Then in his introduction, he made a specific identifying statement for the believers of Sardis: *This is the message from the one who has the sevenfold Spirit of God and the seven stars* (Revelation 3:1b).

[T]he one who has the sevenfold Spirit of God .... Jesus Christ has and is the fullness of the Holy Spirit, or *Spirit of God—sevenfold*, meaning perfection or completion. He is the Triune God, the three in one: Father, Son, and Holy Spirit.

[T]he one who has ... the seven stars .... As we've already seen earlier in the Revelation, *the seven stars* are the seven churches to whom the letters in Revelation 2-3 are written, with these seven churches representative of the entire body of Christ made up of all true believers of all time.

Jesus' introduction is followed by his message to the church in Sardis: *I know all the things you do, and that you have a reputation for being alive—but you are dead. Wake up! Strengthen what little remains, for even what is left is almost dead* (Revelation 3:1c-2a).

Jesus told the Sardis church: *I know all the things you do.* As with each of us, nothing is hidden from God. So even though the church at Sardis had *a reputation for being alive*, the Lord knew better. He said, *you are dead.* What did he mean?

The church at Sardis wasn't undergoing persecution. They were going along and getting along just fine. The church was active and even busy, but it was fitting into its surrounding society so well that the devil had no reason to bother it, which is why Jesus included the warning: *Wake up! Strengthen what little remains, for even what is left is almost dead.*

John Walvoord served as president of Dallas Theological Seminary for more than 30 years. Speaking of Sardis, he described it as a city "ideal for defense, as it ... was surrounded by deep cliffs almost impossible to scale." Even so, Sardis had been conquered twice—once in 549 BC and again in 214 BC. How? Again, I quote Walvoord: "because of overconfidence and failure to watch."

"Overconfidence and failure to watch" had caused Sardis' defeat two times in history, and yet here were God's people making those same foolish mistakes. When Christians begin to rely on past victories or past actions, they're either *dead* or *almost dead.* Every day, believers need a fresh anointing, a fresh word, a fresh enthusiasm for serving the Lord. Sardis had lost theirs, and the Lord wasn't pleased. How fresh is your commitment to Jesus?

Day 25

"Overconfidence and failure to watch" (quoted from John Walvoord's statement about Sardis) had caused Sardis' defeat two times in history, and now the church in that city had developed the same foolish attitude. The church at Sardis was dead: *you have a reputation for being alive—but you are dead* (Revelation 3:1b).

As John MacArthur describes it, the church at Sardis represents the church where "someone cuts the grass, paints the walls, prints the bulletin, and stands in the pulpit. But that church isn't alive; it's dead." Sardis was like the Pharisees Jesus referred to as *whitewashed tombs—beautiful on the outside but filled on the inside with dead people's bones* (Matthew 23:27b).

And Jesus said, *I find that your actions do not meet the requirements of my God* (Revelation 3:2b). Jesus wants to see far more than routine activity in a believer's life. He wants to see the fire and passion of commitment, a burning desire to please him and reach others with the Good News of Jesus. But that's not what the church at Sardis was doing.

Jesus told them: *Go back to what you heard and believed at first; hold to it firmly. Repent and turn to me again. If you don't wake up, I will come to you suddenly, as unexpected as a thief* (Revelation 3:3).

Whether the Lord was warning of his intention to bring judgment on the church at Sardis itself or of his appearance in the Rapture, we can't be sure. Either way, though, he was letting the church at Sardis know what they needed to do: *Go back to what you heard and believed at first; hold to it firmly. Repent and turn to me again.*

But as always, Jesus didn't lump the congregants of the church of Sardis into one mold. Even though sin was rampant in that church, he still knew each person's heart and said: *Yet there are some in the church in Sardis who have not soiled their clothes with evil* (Revelation 3:4a).

The majority of that church may have been *dead*, but there was still a remnant who were faithful. To these Jesus promised: *They will walk with me in white, for they are worthy. All who are victorious will be clothed in white. I will never erase their names from the Book of Life, but I will announce before my Father and his angels that they are mine* (Revelation 3:4b-5).

To those who have truly surrendered to his Lordship, Jesus says: *They will walk with me in white, for they are worthy.* Believers are covered by the righteousness of Christ, making them *worthy* and *victorious* because of his atoning sacrifice.

Here's another huge promise he makes to true believers: *I will never erase their names from the Book of Life, but I will announce before my Father and His angels that they are mine.* In other words, the members of the church in Sardis whose names weren't in *the Book of Life* weren't erased out of the Book because of their sinful behavior. If a name wasn't there, it was because it had never been written in the Book in the first place. Jesus doesn't "pencil in" anybody. The names of his saints are permanently written in blood.

How about your name? Is it written in *the Book of Life*? If it is, you can look forward to the day when you'll hear your Savior announce to his Father, "This one's mine."

Day 26

Sardis was the church whose routine had been going on for so long that Jesus told them: *you have a reputation for being alive—but you are dead. Go back to what you heard and believed at first* (Revelation 3:1b, 3a).

As I said yesterday, the majority of that church may have been *dead*, but there was still a remnant who were faithful. To these Jesus promised: *They will walk with me in white, for they are worthy. All who are victorious will be clothed in white. I will never erase their names from the Book of Life, but I will announce before my Father and his angels that they are mine* (Revelation 3:4b-5).

Jesus taught about this in the Parable of the Weeds. In that lesson, he talked about a farmer who planted seeds which fell on all different sorts of ground. Note what he said about some of these seeds: *Other seeds fell on shallow soil with underlying rock. The seeds sprouted quickly because the soil was shallow. But the plants soon wilted under the hot sun, and since they didn't have deep roots, they died* (Matthew 13:5-6).

Did you get that? *[S]ince they didn't have deep roots, they died.* The farmer, representing Jesus, plants the seeds of the Gospel. But each person makes his own choice as to how they respond. As Jesus explained it: *The seed on the rocky soil represents those who hear the message and immediately receive it with joy. But since they don't have deep roots, they don't last long. They fall away as soon as they have problems or are persecuted for believing God's word* (Matthew 13:20-21).

Like the siblings of my friend I mentioned a few days ago, these folks were all excited about Jesus for a short time. But there had been no conversion. What they had was nothing but surface transformation, not heart transplants.

I can't stress it enough. God has no eraser for the Book of Life. Your name's either in it or not. And the only way to get your name in that Book is through a complete surrender to the Lordship of Jesus.

So what about all these people who say they're saved and then wander off into evil? I'm not their judge and neither are you. But I can guarantee you two things: (1) God will do whatever it takes to get his child's attention, even if that means taking him home rather than letting him continue to embarrass the name of his Father; and (2) God doesn't spank the devil's children. Unless they repent and are adopted into God's family, he will leave their punishment until the Final Judgment.

Just as there were weeds among the good seed in Sardis, there are weeds among the good seed in today's churches. And Jesus plainly tells us what that means: *The enemy who planted the weeds among the wheat is the devil* (Matthew 13:39a). The lost sit in church right alongside the saved.

Be the very best example of Jesus you can possibly be. Others who may not even know him are watching you at church and everywhere else you go.

'Should we pull out the weeds?' they asked. 'No,' he replied, 'you'll uproot the wheat if you do. Let both grow together until the harvest. Then I will tell the harvesters to sort out the weeds, tie them into bundles, and burn them, and to put the wheat in the barn' (Matthew 13:28b-30).

Keep your own doorstep swept clean. Live for Jesus and don't waste time judging others. God will sort us all out when the time comes.

Day 27

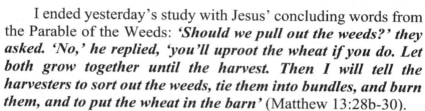

I ended yesterday's study with Jesus' concluding words from the Parable of the Weeds: *'Should we pull out the weeds?' they asked. 'No,' he replied, 'you'll uproot the wheat if you do. Let both grow together until the harvest. Then I will tell the harvesters to sort out the weeds, tie them into bundles, and burn them, and to put the wheat in the barn'* (Matthew 13:28b-30).

So can a truly saved person be lost? Some say "Yes" and some say "No." David messed up big-time with his adulterous relationship with Bathsheeba. Moses took credit for God's miracle of water from the rock at Meribah, even hitting the rock twice with his rod when God had instructed him to simply speak to the rock (see Numbers 20). Moses got to see the Promised Land but wasn't allowed to enter it because of his disobedience. Both of these occurrences, though, were pre-grace, pre-cross, and pre-resurrection.

Yet there are many New Testament scriptures that leave you wondering. Take for example when Jesus refers to himself as *the vine* (John 15:5a) and people as *the branches* (John 15:5b). He says: *Remain in me, and I will remain in you* (John 15:4a).

This is by no means all-encompassing, but here are the three main schools of thought regarding salvation: (1) You are saved through faith in Jesus Christ. Once you're adopted into the Kingdom, Jesus will never kick you out of his family. (2) You are saved through faith in Jesus Christ and adopted into his family; however, some actions warrant being booted out of the family, thus losing your salvation. (3) You are saved through faith in Jesus Christ and adopted into his family. However, you may one day decide you just don't believe any of that Jesus stuff anymore and choose to denounce him, thus giving up your salvation. In other words, no one can or will take away your salvation, but you can make the choice to give it up.

I'm not about to say that any of these viewpoints are right or wrong because I think if you're serious about living for Jesus, you're not going to be looking for loopholes in your contract! The Bible makes it clear that some people come into the church *disguised as harmless sheep but are really vicious wolves* (Matthew 7:15b). These are unquestionably imposters, fake Christians who are intent upon destroying the harmony within the church body and pulling real believers away from the truth.

I suggest we don't waste time trying to figure out who's real and who isn't. That time can be much better spent doing the work of the Kingdom. As we saw yesterday, Jesus is prepared to sort everyone out at the Final Judgment. Get out there and be wheat for the Bread of Life.

Day 28

Philadelphia is the sixth of the seven churches to which Jesus instructed John to write. Let's take a look at the entire letter before expounding on any of its content:

Write this letter to the angel of the church in Philadelphia: This is the message from the one who is holy and true, the one who has the key of David. What he opens, no one can close; and what he closes, no one can open:

I know all the things you do, and I have opened a door for you that no one can close. You have little strength, yet you obeyed my word and did not deny me. Look, I will force those who belong to Satan's synagogue—those liars who say they are Jews but are not—to come and bow down at your feet. They will acknowledge that you are the ones I love.

Because you have obeyed my command to persevere, I will protect you from the great time of testing that will come upon the whole world to test those who belong to this world. I am coming soon. Hold on to what you have, so that no one will take away your crown. All who are victorious will become pillars in the Temple of my God, and they will never have to leave it. And I will write on them the name of my God, and they will be citizens in the city of my God—the New Jerusalem that comes down from heaven from my God. And I will also write on them my new name.

Anyone with ears to hear must listen to the Spirit and understand what he is saying to the churches (Revelation 3:7-13).

The church at Philadelphia, like the church of Ephesus, was doing everything right. They were doing good, steering clear of evil, and making sure no false doctrines crept in. But where the Ephesians failed to grow in love for Christ and others, the Philadelphians abounded in it. And because of their faithfulness, Jesus told them: ***I have opened a door for you that no one can close*** (Revelation 3:8b). They were a healthy congregation, feeding the flock within and reaching outside the church with the love and the Good News of Jesus.

What a blessing-filled promise Jesus makes to the church of Philadelphia! He tells these faithful servants: ***What he opens, no one can close; and what he closes, no one can open.***

Are you a faithful servant of Jesus Christ? If so, this promise is for you. More on this passage tomorrow.

Day 29

How does Jesus identify Himself to the church at Philadelphia? *This is the message from the one who is holy and true, the one who has the key of David. What he opens, no one can close; and what he closes, no one can open* (Revelation 3:7b).

This is the message from the one who is holy and true. Who is *holy*? God and God alone. Jesus is identifying himself as God. And not just any "god." The God. The True God. The One and Only.

[T]he one who has the key of David. Jesus is quoting from Isaiah: *I will give him the key to the house of David—the highest position in the royal court. When he opens doors, no one will be able to close them; when he closes doors, no one will be able to open them* (Isaiah 22:22). The Christians in Philadelphia were undoubtedly familiar with this passage and would understand its tremendous significance regarding Jesus' identity. Why?

Because look at Jesus' next words to Philadelphia: *I know all the things you do, and I have opened a door for you that no one can close. You have little strength, yet you obeyed my word and did not deny me* (Revelation 3:8).

When we looked at the church in Smyrna, I said it was the only one of the seven churches that received a clean bill of health. Philadelphia comes close, but notice what the Lord said: *You have little strength.* God's strength is unlimited. God's resources are unlimited. Perhaps this was a mild chastisement for relying too much on themselves.

Even so, under tough circumstances, the Philadelphian

Christians had remained faithful. And because of their faithfulness, the Lord told them he had **opened a door ... that no one can close.** Their opportunities to witness for the Lord and expand his Kingdom were wide open.

Have you ever seen one of those shows or been to one of those "locked room" adventures where a person has to find his way out of what seems to be a completely sealed room? This may be how the Philadelphians felt. Their **little strength** may not have seemed like much. They may have looked around their city filled with pagan gods and failed to see the opportunities before them. But Jesus said to look more closely.

I've spoken about this experience many times, but it bears repeating. While in the checkout line at a department store, I began to pray for an opportunity to witness to the cashier, who was clearly having a very bad day. I just hoped to cheer her up a bit. I didn't expect the wide open door that the Lord gave me.

When I simply asked, "How are you?" she looked me straight in the face and said, "You want to know the truth? I want to die." The condensed version of what happened after that is that she took her break and told me that her husband had left her and that she was suicidal. I told her about a Man I could prove to her in writing would **never leave you or forsake you** (Hebrews 13:5b, HCSB). And because of a simple "How are you?" a new member was added to the family of God and a hopeless woman came to know Real Hope.

Like the church at Philadelphia, the opportunities may not be staring you in the face, but especially in these last days, the Lord has swung wide the doors of evangelism. Through Facebook, Twitter, Instagram, email, TV, radio, books, ebooks, phones, and more, ways and means of telling others about Jesus are everywhere. Even face-to-face and eyeball-to-eyeball.

Look for and pray for your own opportunities—what David Wilkerson calls "divine appointments"—to tell others about Jesus. Show His love in the way you talk and act toward others. Even a **little strength** is battle-winning power when it's entrusted to the mighty hands of Jesus.

Day 30

We're looking at the sixth letter of Jesus in the Book of Revelation. He tells John to write to the church in Philadelphia. These believers, even under tough circumstances, had remained faithful, so Jesus gave them this promise: *Because you have obeyed my command to persevere, I will protect you from the great time of testing that will come upon the whole world to test those who belong to this world* (Revelation 3:10).

As we've already learned, although some Bible scholars see the seven letters to the churches as representative of different church ages, the majority of scholars believe—and I concur—that these letters encompass Jesus' message to the entire church of the Living Christ—each and every true believer who is living now and those who have already gone on before us. From that viewpoint, it's easy to figure out what *great time of testing* Jesus was talking about.

At a point coming up soon in Jesus' Revelation, the entire True Church will be removed from this world and taken to be with Jesus. At that time, the Tribulation will begin and will include horrific persecution of God's people. But if God's people are taken away in the Rapture, how can God's people be the ones being persecuted? Here's how Jesus explains it the book of Luke:

Yes, it will be 'business as usual' right up to the day when the Son of Man is revealed.... [T]wo people will be asleep in one bed; one will be taken, the other left. Two women will be grinding flour together at the mill; one will be taken, the other left (Luke 17:30, 34-35).

Don't misunderstand this passage. Jesus, ***the Son of Man***, isn't going to choose one person to take and leave another behind. At whatever point Jesus returns for his Church, those decisions will have already been made by each person's individual choice. Those who committed their lives to Jesus will be taken in the Rapture. Those who have not will be left behind. And many who are left behind will realize what has happened, repent, and commit their lives to Jesus, but they will pay a terrible price for having waited until after the Rapture.

I can't overstress this: church membership is not a ticket to heaven. Only a genuine, sold-out commitment to Jesus Christ will get you there.

The Lord, speaking through the prophet Jeremiah, warns: ***In all history there has never been such a time of terror*** (Jeremiah 30:7a). Jesus told the church at Philadelphia they would miss out on this time. He tells the faithful today the same thing.

So what purpose will this terrible time serve? It ***will come upon the whole world to test those who belong to this world.*** Anyone who hasn't committed their life to Jesus belongs ***to this world.*** And this terrible time will be their last opportunity to turn to Jesus.

If he returned today, would you be ready? If he returned today, who among your family and friends would be going with Jesus? If you haven't already committed your life to Jesus, do it now. And if you've already done that, talk to your friends and family about the importance and urgency to make that same commitment.

[N]ow is the time to seek the Lord (Hosea 10:12b).

Day 31

All who are victorious will become pillars in the Temple of my God, and they will never have to leave it. And I will write on them the name of my God, and they will be citizens in the city of my God—the New Jerusalem that comes down from heaven from my God. And I will also write on them my new name (Revelation 3:12).

Good News! Good News! The faithful believers in the church in Philadelphia were commended by the Lord and promised deliverance *from the great time of testing* (Revelation 3:10) that would be coming on the world. As we've already seen, this message was not only for the Philadelphian church, but for all true believers from then until right this very minute. Jesus promises to keep us *from the great time of testing* by removing all his people from this world prior to the Great Tribulation.

But there's more Good News for believers. We'll have a permanent new home: *All who are victorious will become pillars in the Temple of my God, and they will never have to leave it.* We'll *be citizens in the city of my God—the New Jerusalem that comes down from heaven from my God.*

What else? We'll be permanent members of the family of God: *And I will write on them the name of my God.... And I will also write on them my new name.*

When the Lord takes us out of this world, we're going to know him as he knows us. Completely. Totally. We will come into a full understanding of *the mind of Christ* (2 Corinthians 2:16b). Talk about amazing grace!

As with the other messages to the churches, Jesus closed Philadelphia's letter with these words: ***Anyone with ears to hear must listen to the Spirit and understand what he is saying to the churches*** (Revelation 3:13).

There is tremendous urgency in these messages. Be prepared! Be ready! Are you? And are you helping others prepare for his coming?

Day 32

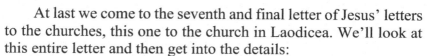

At last we come to the seventh and final letter of Jesus' letters to the churches, this one to the church in Laodicea. We'll look at this entire letter and then get into the details:

Write this letter to the angel of the church in Laodicea. This is the message from the one who is the Amen—the faithful and true witness, the beginning of God's new creation:

I know all the things you do, that you are neither hot nor cold. I wish that you were one or the other! But since you are like lukewarm water, neither hot nor cold, I will spit you out of my mouth! You say, 'I am rich. I have everything I want. I don't need a thing!' And you don't realize that you are wretched and miserable and poor and blind and naked. So I advise you to buy gold from me—gold that has been purified by fire. Then you will be rich. Also buy white garments from me so you will not be shamed by your nakedness, and ointment for your eyes so you will be able to see. I correct and discipline everyone I love. So be diligent and turn from your indifference.

Look! I stand at the door and knock. If you hear my voice and open the door, I will come in, and we will share a meal together as friends. Those who are victorious will sit with me on my throne, just as I was victorious and sat with my Father on his throne. Anyone with ears to hear must listen to the Spirit and understand what he is saying to the churches (Revelation 3:14-22).

See how Jesus identified himself in this letter to the church in Laodicea*: the one who is the Amen—the faithful and true witness, the beginning of God's new creation.* He called himself *the faithful and true witness* because he intends to show the contrast between his faithfulness and the believers or professing believers of Laodicea who were anything but *faithful and true.*

And what about *the beginning of God's new creation*? There is nothing *new* about Jesus. He is *the Lord God, the Almighty—the one who always was, who is, and who is still to come* (Revelation 4:8b). He is the Great *I Am* (Exodus 3:14).

As the Berean Study Bible words Revelation 3:14, Jesus is *the Originator of God's creation.* I think this is the best and clearest translation of all. It is absolutely critical to realize Jesus is not a created being. He is the Creator.

As John described him: *In the beginning was the Word, and the Word was with God, and the Word was God. He was with God in the beginning. Through him all things were made, and without him nothing was made that has been made* (John 1:1-3).

And he has a lot to say to the church of Laodicea. And that same message is for us today. Jesus wants us to be like him: *faithful and true.*

Day 33

The city of Laodicea had no local water source. Its water was supplied through a six-mile long series of pipes or troughs that began at a hot springs in Hierapolis. This channel then depended on gravity for the water to flow into Laodicea. This system was called an aqueduct—*aque* as in *water*, and *duct* which comes from the same root word as our modern word *conduct*. In other words, the aqueduct conducted or channeled the water from the springs into the city of Laodicea.

And when it got there, boy, was it tasty! Think about water from a hot springs that has traveled far enough to cool down but still be pretty warm. Lukewarm. No wonder Jesus spoke as he did to the Laodiceans. They completely understood what he meant when he said, *I know all the things you do, that you are neither hot nor cold. I wish that you were one or the other!*

When it comes to drinking water, there are times when a nice cold drink sure hits the spot, but there are also occasions when hot water comes in handy. But lukewarm? Uh-uh. Nobody likes lukewarm. Not even Jesus. So he tells them: *But since you are like lukewarm water, neither hot nor cold, I will spit you out of my mouth!*

Laodicea's water had to be tough to stomach. The behavior of the church at Laodicea was equally disgusting. This was the church that had gone so far from the teachings of the Word of God that even though his name may have been invoked on occasion, the true Lord Jesus Christ had no place whatsoever within it. Its erroneous teachings had made it not a church, but a cult that denied the true Gospel and sprinkled in a little of this and that.

This was the church that made Jesus want to throw up.

I will spit you out of my mouth! The original language here is so descriptive. Jesus isn't saying, "You make me want to gag." He's saying in modern-day language, "You make me want to spew." The word for *spit* denotes the image of projectile vomiting. Jesus didn't have or want any part in that lukewarm congregation.

His opinion on lukewarmness hasn't changed. He still despises it. Yet how many of us are best described as *lukewarm*? We aren't all excited about loving Jesus and serving him and others. But we're not ice cold, either. We're just plugging along, with no thought for our own spiritual state or the condition of anyone else. Even though all seven of Jesus' letters to the churches are directed at all churches in all ages right up to today, I think the Laodiceans describe the majority of Christians today. And I can't be honest without saying I fall right in with them on many occasions.

How would Jesus describe you—hot, cold, or lukewarm?

Day 34

In His seventh and final letter to the churches, Jesus has already told the church at Laodicea that their lukewarmness made him want to vomit. He continues to speak the truth to this bunch of phony believers:

You say, 'I am rich. I have everything I want. I don't need a thing!' And you don't realize that you are wretched and miserable and poor and blind and naked (Revelation 3:17).

Laodicea was a wealthy city. They were known for the production of fancy textiles and their medical school which was associated with the temple of the healing god Asklepios. They were a proud and confident people. But the Lord let them know their material possessions meant nothing in the Kingdom of God. He saw them as they really were.

That's why he tells them: *So I advise you to buy gold from me—gold that has been purified by fire. Then you will be rich. Also buy white garments from me so you will not be shamed by your nakedness, and ointment for your eyes so you will be able to see* (Revelation 3:18).

Money and fancy clothes didn't hide the fact that these professing Christians were, as my friend Gwen's mama would have said, "as naked as picked birds" when it came to anything in God's Kingdom. They, like the *blind Pharisee* Jesus referred to in Matthew 23:26, may have put on the appearance of being a church, but the fact was that they were as lost as proverbial ducks in the desert. They all needed Jesus. Which is why this is where we read: *Look! I stand at the door and knock* (Revelation 3:20a).

Jesus wasn't in that church. Jesus wasn't in the hearts of these professing believers. They, like the Pharisees Jesus had chastised, did not belong to the Kingdom. But he didn't want to leave them in their lost state. He told them: *If you hear my voice and open the door, I will come in, and we will share a meal together as friends. Those who are victorious will sit with me on my throne, just as I was victorious and sat with my Father on his throne* (Revelation 3:20b-21).

Jesus died for all: *For God so loved the world* (John 3:16a, KJV). But He loves us enough to give us freedom of choice. His Holy Spirit will knock repeatedly on the doors of our hearts, but he won't force us to let him in. We must choose to open our hearts to him.

When any person welcomes Jesus Christ into their heart, that person is welcomed into the Kingdom. He becomes *victorious*. He has a home in heaven.

Do you know where your eternal home will be? Are you serious about serving Jesus? Time is short. Don't waste it.

Day 35

As we saw yesterday, the people of the church of Laodicea were phonies. While they grouped together and called themselves a church, their teachings had strayed completely away from the Gospel, and Jesus was nowhere to be found within their congregation. He was outside, standing at the door and knocking (see Revelation 3:20a).

If the professing Christians of Laodicea weren't members of God's family, why does he include this church among his letters? To warn them and to warn congregations in all ages, including today.

Many churches today are churches in name only. Laodicea's erroneous teachings had made it not a church, but a cult that denied the true Gospel and merely sprinkled in a little bit of Christian teaching. There are a lot of Laodicean churches out there today.

What do I mean? I could give plenty of examples, but one of the biggest is the "feel-good" church. Their "gospel" is that God wants everybody to be healthy and wealthy. That's a lie. I've been in legal and illegal churches in China and I've met some remarkably dedicated Christians. Poor as can be. Under constant danger of arrest or worse. Yet their joy overflows.

What did the Apostle Paul say about the churches in Macedonia? ***They are being tested by many troubles, and they are very poor*** (2 Corinthians 8:2a). The Kingdom of God is not about being trouble-free, pain-free, or loaded with money and material things. If you're listening to a name-it-and-claim-it preacher, cut it out. He or she is leading you away from the teachings of the Bible.

God forbid that anyone reading this is part of a Laodicean church. Those churches will still be here when Jesus calls his people out of this world. This is the church that will lead countless numbers into hell and, before the Final Judgment, will survive and possibly even thrive during the Tribulation.

Let me say it one more time before we move from these letters into the next part of the Revelation. Church membership gets no one into heaven. There is no action anyone can take on behalf of someone else that will get that person into heaven. Every individual must make his own decision to personally and sincerely confess his need for a Savior and surrender his life wholly to Jesus Christ.

Want to miss out on the Tribulation? Commit your life to Jesus now.

Revelation 4

Day 36

We've just completed a look at the seven letters Jesus dictated to John that were to be delivered to seven churches in Asia Minor.

Now we move from an earthly viewpoint to a heavenly one. Remember, Jesus had told John to **Write down what you have seen—both the things that are now happening and the things that will happen** (Revelation 1:19). John's next words show us the transition: **After this I looked, and there before me was a door standing open in heaven. And the voice I had first heard speaking to me like a trumpet said, 'Come up here, and I will show you what must take place after this'** (Revelation 4:1, NIV).

After this ... After what? After writing down all seven of Jesus' letters to the churches. John not only saw an open doorway into heaven, he also heard once again **the voice I had first heard.** What voice? When? At the beginning of John's vision: **It was the Lord's Day, and I was worshiping in the Spirit. Suddenly, I heard behind me a loud voice like a trumpet blast** (Revelation 1:10).

Who does that voice belong to? He's already identified himself: **'I am the Alpha and the Omega—the beginning and the end,' says the Lord God. 'I am the one who is, who always was, and who is still to come—the Almighty One'** (Revelation 1:8).

Jesus himself is speaking and Jesus himself is extending this amazing invitation: *Come up here, and I will show you what must happen after this.* From this point forward, John sees a heavenly perspective of future events.

And instantly I was in the Spirit (Revelation 4:2a). As we saw at the beginning of the Revelation, John has already said he was *worshiping in the Spirit*. John may have been *worshiping in the Spirit*, but physically he was still on the Isle of Patmos.

But when Jesus told John to *Come up here*, John was transported either in spirit or possibly even physically into the realms of heaven. Remember Paul's experience? In 2 Corinthians 12:2, he said: *I was caught up to the third heaven fourteen years ago. Whether I was in my body or out of my body, I don't know—only God knows.*

However Paul's or John's experience took place, it was amazing! And John begins to see what takes place when he, as a member of the body of Christ—which is the Church—is taken out of this world and into heaven. Revelation 4:1 marks the point at which all true believers are removed from this world in what we call the Rapture. What happens after that are end-time events after the Church is removed from Planet Earth.

Fasten your seat belts. We're taking off on an exciting journey!

Day 37

Revelation 4 opens with John telling us of Jesus' invitation for him to see the end-time events from a heavenly perspective. From this point forward, there is no more mention of the Church. Why? Most Bible scholars believe that the True Church has been taken out of the world at this point. In other words, the Rapture has occurred. Those who have truly committed their hearts and lives to Jesus will have been removed from Planet Earth before the things John is about to describe take place.

Remember Jesus' words to the faithful believers of Philadelphia? *Because you have obeyed my command to persevere, I will protect you from the great time of testing that will come upon the whole world to test those who belong to this world* (Revelation 3:10). This is his promise to all who belong to Jesus: they will miss out on *the great time of testing*, also known as the Tribulation.

Then John does his best to describe his first glimpse of heaven. But everything he sees is beyond the scope of human imagining, far greater than mere human words can express. As Paul put it after his own experience, he *heard things that can't be expressed in words, things that humans cannot put into words* (2 Corinthians 12:4). But John tries his best to share with us what he experienced. For now, we'll only look at the latter half of verse 2: *I saw a throne in heaven and someone sitting on it* (Revelation 4:2b).

The first thing John sees is *a throne*. What's significant about *a throne*? It's the place of supreme authority, but it's more than that: it's the resting place of supreme authority.

Mark 16:19 tells us that after Jesus met with the disciples and gave them the Great Commission, he *was taken up into heaven and sat down in the place of honor.* Why is it so important that Jesus *sat down*? Because his work was finished, just as he said from the cross (see John 19:30).

So our view of heaven opens with *a throne*. But not just any throne. It's an occupied throne. The Supreme Authority has completed his work *and sat down in the place of honor.*

Which brings us to an important fact: every person has someone or something enthroned as their object of worship. For some, it's worldly wealth. Material possessions. Prestige. Even self. For others, the most important thing in their lives may be their spouses or children or grandchildren. Whatever is most important to you sits enthroned over your life. And for every believer, that place should belong to Jesus. No thing or person should ever take a higher place of importance than the Lord Jesus.

If you can't truly say Jesus has first place in your life, it's time to change your priorities. By putting Christ above all else—including your spouse, kids, grandkids, self, or even your parents—you'll become a better spouse or parent or grandparent or son or daughter. You'll become a better everything.

Tomorrow we'll get into John's description of the glorified Jesus.

Day 38

We've just begun our look at Revelation 4 and Jesus has extended the amazing invitation for John to join him in heaven and see the end-time events from a heavenly perspective. From this point forward, the church is no longer mentioned because, in my and many far more learned Bible scholars' opinions, the Church has been taken out of the world and won't experience the things Jesus is about to reveal. But before we see the view from heaven to Earth, we get an astounding look at the glorified Christ, seated on his throne: *The one sitting on the throne was as brilliant as gemstones—like jasper and carnelian. And the glow of an emerald circled his throne like a rainbow* (Revelation 4:3).

Remember, John is doing his best to describe the indescribable. Any descriptions we read in Revelation are far less than what is actually seen. John simply had no better words with which to describe what he saw.

John has zero words to describe Jesus himself, so he tells us of the brilliant light emanating from the glorified Christ—*jasper*, like a diamond. Pure white. And *carnelian*, blood red. Here we see the purity of Jesus and the precious price he paid for all who will believe in him. The light around the throne formed an arc John calls *a rainbow*, but it's a single color: green, glowing *like an emerald*. The color green signifies life. Hope.

The arc or rainbow shape reminds us of God's promise spoken to Noah in Genesis 9:12-16 after the flood: *I am giving you a sign of my covenant with you and with all living creatures, for all generations to come. I have placed my rainbow in the clouds. It is the sign of my covenant with you and with all the*

77

earth. When I send clouds over the earth, the rainbow will appear in the clouds, and I will remember my covenant with you and with all living creatures. Never again will the floodwaters destroy all life. When I see the rainbow in the clouds, I will remember the eternal covenant between God and every living creature on earth.

Jesus on his throne is the Ultimate Authority. He has All Power. And yet everything John sees lets him know that this glorified Christ is the same Promise Keeper whom John knew in his earthly body. What did Jesus say in John 10:10b? *I am come that they might have life, and that they might have it more abundantly* (KJV).

Judgment is necessary. The final destruction of all evil is necessary. But what joy awaits those who have repented of evil and live for Jesus! Want a life of real abundance? Live for Jesus.

We'll see a bit more of heaven tomorrow.

Day 39

Either in the Spirit or even physically, too, John has entered heaven and seen the glorified Christ. The emerald or green arc or rainbow around Jesus signified the life and hope found only in him. When Ezekiel was given a vision of the Lord, he described a similar scene as did John. He saw *something that looked like a throne made of blue lapis lazuli. And on this throne high above was a figure whose appearance resembled a man. From what appeared to be his waist up, he looked like gleaming amber, flickering like a fire. And from his waist down, he looked like a burning flame, shining with splendor. All around him was a glowing halo, like a rainbow shining in the clouds on a rainy day. This is what the glory of the Lord looked like to me* (Ezekiel 1:26b-28a).

Jesus Christ is the glory of God. As the writer of Hebrews so clearly states, *The Son radiates God's own glory and expresses the very character of God* (Hebrews 1:3a). John's description continues: *Twenty-four thrones surrounded him, and twenty-four elders sat on them. They were all clothed in white and had gold crowns on their heads* (Revelation 4:4).

Who were these *elders*? Here again there's a debate among Bible scholars, but from the materials I've read, I choose to believe these 24 people are representative of all the people who belong to Christ: 12, being a number of completeness, represents the Old Testament believers, and 12 represents the New Testament believers all the way into today. In other words, the One True Church surrounds the throne of God.

Three things we're told about these *elders*:

(1) They're *clothed in white*. Take a look at the words of Isaiah: *I am overwhelmed with joy in the Lord my God! For He has dressed me with the clothing of salvation and draped me in a robe of righteousness. I am like a bridegroom in his wedding suit or a bride with her jewels* (Isaiah 61:10). Jesus himself clothes his people in his own righteousness.

(2) They're wearing *gold crowns on their heads*. Some passages in the Bible show us angels robed in white, but you'll never read where an angel is wearing a crown. A crown indicates authority. Jesus' people will share his authority. As 2 Timothy 2:12 reminds us, true believers *will reign with him.*

(3) Which is why we see these *elders* sitting on *thrones*. Ephesians 3:6a says, *And this is God's plan: Both Gentiles and Jews who believe the Good News share equally in the riches inherited by God's children.* Jesus Christ has one people, made up of all who believed in the promise of the Messiah and all who have believed in him after his death, burial, and resurrection.

Robed in white. Crowned with his glory. Ruling and reigning with Jesus. The privileges of the redeemed are astounding. Don't miss out.

Day 40

We're looking at Revelation 4 where John has been invited by the Lord Jesus into heaven to see future events from a heavenly viewpoint. Already, John has seen Jesus on his throne and the 24 elders surrounding him on their thrones. He continues his description: *From the throne came flashes of lightning and the rumble of thunder. And in front of the throne were seven torches with burning flames. This is the sevenfold Spirit of God* (Revelation 4:5).

[F]lashes of lightning and the rumble of thunder. In Exodus, we read where the Lord announced the Ten Commandments to the people of Israel at Mount Sinai. He had told Moses, *I will come to you in a thick cloud, Moses, so the people themselves can hear me when I speak with you. Then they will always trust you* (Exodus 19:9). And as he spoke, lightning and thunder emanated from the dark cloud that hid his glory.

When the people heard the thunder and the loud blast of the ram's horn, and when they saw the flashes of lightning and the smoke billowing from the mountain, they stood at a distance, trembling with fear (Exodus 20:18).

Now here's John face-to-face with the glorified Savior. We can't even imagine the awe of the scene before him. Along with the thunder and lightning, he saw that *in front of the throne were seven torches with burning flames. This is the sevenfold Spirit of God.* When the Lord began giving the Revelation to John, this was his opening statement: *Grace and peace to you from the one who is, who always was, and who is still to come; from the sevenfold Spirit before his throne* (Revelation 1:4).

81

[T]he sevenfold Spirit before his throne and the *seven torches with burning flames* were the Holy Spirit. The Holy Spirit is God. No, we can't see him, but those who know him can surely feel his presence, guidance, and love. Everything Jesus is, everything God is, the Holy Spirit also is.

Our attitude toward the Holy Spirit reminds me of the little girl who was afraid of the dark. Her mother told her, "Don't be scared. The Holy Spirit is with you."

"I know," the little girl responded, "but I want somebody with skin on 'em."

That's us so much of the time. We have no problem believing that an image will appear on our TV screen when we press the power button. We believe our car will go when we press the accelerator and stop when we press the brake. Think of all we do with a cell phone, without even thinking. Or a computer. We don't understand how any of these things work, and yet we have total confidence in them.

We can't see the Holy Spirit, but he is much more real than any of the things I just named. And surely the God of the Universe deserves more of our confidence than a bunch of gadgets.

He is God. If you belong to Jesus, he is with you. Live like Jesus is in the room. Because he is.

Day 41

Let me remind you that from the opening of Revelation 4 when John is invited to *Come up here* (Revelation 1:1), there is no further mention of the Church because the Church has already been taken out of the world and into glory.

John tries to describe what he sees in heaven, including *[t]he one sitting on the throne*, the 24 elders and their thrones, and the seven torches he sees *in front of the throne*, which he identifies as *the sevenfold Spirit of God* (from Revelation 4:3-5).

In front of the throne was a shiny sea of glass, sparkling like crystal (Revelation 4:6a)—we'll see this sea again in Revelation 15:2. What is this *sea of glass*? John offers no explanation or details, but it seems to be reminiscent of the *sea of brass* we read about in 1 Kings 7:23-26. When King Solomon built the Temple, this laver, or wash basin, was made 18 feet in diameter and held 16,000 gallons of water. Huge. It was for washing the priests' hands and feet in preparation for certain ceremonies or duties (see Exodus 30:18-21). So it's safe to say the *sea of glass* is in some way related to cleansing.

The book of Jude closes with these two verses: *Now to him who is able to preserve you without sin, and to present you spotless before the presence of his glory with exceeding joy, in the coming of our Lord Jesus Christ, To the only God our Saviour through Jesus Christ our Lord, be glory and magnificence, empire and power, before all ages, and now, and for all ages of ages. Amen* (Jude 1:24-25, Douay-Rheims Bible).

In my opinion, the *sea of glass* represents the cleansing of the believer. Each of us will one day stand before Jesus, either to be welcomed into his Kingdom or to be sentenced to eternal separation from him. (The condemned will stand before the Great White Throne of Judgment—see Revelation 20:11-15.)

Those who have accepted his sacrifice and received him as Lord and Savior will stand *spotless before the presence of his glory*, no doubt *with exceeding joy*. I pray everyone reading this will be among that number.

Day 42

In the center and around the throne were four living beings, each covered with eyes, front and back. The first of these living beings was like a lion; the second was like an ox; the third had a human face; and the fourth was like an eagle in flight. Each of these living beings had six wings, and their wings were covered all over with eyes, inside and out. Day after day and night after night they keep on saying, 'Holy, holy, holy is the Lord God, the Almighty—the one who always was, who is, and who is still to come' (Revelation 4:6b-8).

[F]our living beings circle *around the throne* of the glorified Jesus Christ. Their descriptions include attributes similar to a lion, an ox, a human, and an eagle. All of them are praising God. This reminds me of Psalm 96:13a, *Let all creation rejoice before the Lord* (NIV).

But there's much more to these four very interesting figures. To see that, we first need to look at Ezekiel 1:5-24. I hope you'll take time to read that entire passage. In Ezekiel's vision, he sees these same four beings and says that *each had four faces* (Ezekiel 1:6a). John's description gives us the idea that these figures differed in appearance. However, Ezekiel makes it clear that all four beings were identical, with each possessing all four faces.

It's important to also note here that while the KJV refers to these *beings* as *beasts*, that's a poor translation. What are they? Cherubim, the plural of the word cherub. Instead of the chubby, naked, little winged angels we see in cartoons, the Bible describes

85

cherubim as powerful and super-intelligent. Just how powerful and intelligent? Ezekiel 28:14 tells us that Satan (Lucifer) was *an anointed guardian cherub* (ESV).

John also says: *Each of these living beings had six wings, and their wings were covered all over with eyes, inside and out.* Eyes indicate understanding, so these beings are a whole lot smarter than any human and see everything much more clearly than we do. Add to that the fact that they're in the very presence of the glorified Lord, and we realize just how important these *living beings* are.

And their faces? The lion is pretty easy to figure out, since Jesus *is the lion of the tribe of Judah* (Revelation 5:5a). In Numbers 2, we see where the 12 tribes were divided into four groups around the tabernacle during the Israelites' time in the wilderness. The group headed by Judah had, of course, a lion as its emblem; Ephraim, an ox; Reuben, a man; and Dan, an eagle.

Whether or not those tribal emblems are related to the faces we see on the cherubim isn't the most important point here, though. What is? The singular focus of these *four living beings*. They are in awe of Jesus. And so should we be.

Holy, holy, holy is the Lord God, the Almighty—the one who always was, who is, and who is still to come.

Day 43

As we saw yesterday, the four living beings, or cherubim, around the throne of the glorified Christ are constantly praising their Creator. But that's only the praise of the cherubim. Psalm 96:13a says: *Let all creation rejoice before the Lord* (NIV). So what is happening with the 24 elders on their thrones around the Savior?

Whenever the living beings give glory and honor and thanks to the one sitting on the throne (the one who lives forever and ever), the twenty-four elders fall down and worship the one sitting on the throne (the one who lives forever and ever). And they lay their crowns before the throne and say, 'You are worthy, O Lord our God, to receive glory and honor and power. For you created all things, and they exist because you created what you pleased' (Revelation 4:9-11).

They're also worshiping Jesus! And don't miss this: they *fall down and worship*. I realize a lot of folks are physically unable to kneel when praying or worshiping, but I highly recommend you try it if you're still able. You'll never see a Muslim worship Allah kicked back in his seat or standing. No, he's on his face in worship. Surely the Lord Jesus Christ deserves this much honor and more.

Notice, too, that the elders *lay their crowns before the throne*. How'd they get those crowns? Paul has the answer in 2 Timothy 4:8: *And now the prize awaits me—the crown of righteousness, which the Lord, the righteous Judge, will give me on the day of his return. And the prize is not just for me but for all who eagerly look forward to his appearing.*

The word for *crown* used in 2 Timothy 4:8 and in Revelation 4:10 is the Greek word *stephanos*. This is the kind of crown that was given to the winners in an athletic competition. This is a crown of victory. And by laying those crowns at the feet of Jesus, the redeemed are acknowledging that they didn't earn those crowns, but that they were bestowed on them only because of what Jesus did on their behalf.

Laying their crowns at Jesus' feet was an easily understandable image for those living in John's day. A ruler would generally have a number of lesser kings serving under him. Whenever these minor kings were called before the chief ruler or king, they would bow down and present their crowns to him. This was their way of saying, "Any authority we have is only because you allow us to have it." The chief ruler would then return the crowns to the minor kings, letting them know that he appreciated their acknowledgment of his supreme authority and that he was again bestowing his own authority on them.

This is what's happening with the elders we see around Christ's throne. They are acknowledging that they earned nothing but are there and crowned with Christ's righteousness and none of their own.

Do you *eagerly look forward to his appearing*? If so, your *crown of righteousness* awaits!

Revelation 5

Day 44

Now we come to Chapter 5: *Then I saw a scroll in the right hand of the one who was sitting on the throne. There was writing on the inside and the outside of the scroll, and it was sealed with seven seals. And I saw a strong angel, who shouted with a loud voice: 'Who is worthy to break the seals on this scroll and open it?' But no one in heaven or on earth or under the earth was able to open the scroll and read it.*

Then I began to weep bitterly because no one was found worthy to open the scroll and read it. But one of the twenty-four elders said to me, 'Stop weeping! Look, the Lion of the tribe of Judah, the heir to David's throne, has won the victory. He is worthy to open the scroll and its seven seals' (Revelation 5:1-5).

Revelation gets a bit confusing because of all the symbolism, but hang in there and we'll pick this apart and make it understandable. John's focus in this passage is *a scroll in the right hand of the one who was sitting on the throne*. This scroll had *writing on the inside and the outside*. Normally a scroll only had writing on one side, but this scroll had writing on both sides. Thus, this scroll contained an unusual amount of information.

Notice something else unusual about this scroll. Instead of being sealed with one seal, it was sealed with seven. Typically, seven seals were used to seal a will, which seems totally appropriate considering that every word was the absolute will of God. In a human will, we are expressing our wish or will that certain things take place, as in our house going to this person or money going to that person. In this scroll, the Eternal God's will or plan is announced.

Who's holding this scroll? The glorified Christ. Yet this powerful unidentified angel calls out, *Who is worthy to break the seals on this scroll and open it?* And no one answers. Not even Jesus. In that pause, John begins to cry because he senses the importance of the information contained within the scroll and wants to know what it says.

That's when one of the 24 elders, the representatives of the One True Church of all ages, comforts John and tells him: *Look, the Lion of the tribe of Judah, the heir to David's throne, has won the victory. He is worthy to open the scroll and its seven seals.*

Then I saw a Lamb that looked as if it had been slaughtered, but it was now standing between the throne and the four living beings and among the twenty-four elders (Revelation 5:6a).

The Lion of the tribe of Judah is announced as *worthy to open the scroll*, and yet when John looks, he sees *a Lamb*. A delicate, gentle Lamb. And it *looked as if it had been slaughtered*. The Lamb of God bore the scars of his sacrifice.

And look where the Lamb is: *standing . . . among the twenty-four elders*. Remember, the 24 elders represent the One True Church. Everything Jesus went through, he did for the Church. His Bride. His children. His people.

"Oh, how He loves you and me, Oh, how He loves you and me. He gave his life, what more could He give? Oh, how He loves you; Oh, how He loves me; Oh, how He loves you and me" (Word Music, 1975).

Day 45

Here are the highlights of what we looked at yesterday: *Then I saw a scroll in the right hand of the one who was sitting on the throne ... 'Who is worthy to break the seals on this scroll and open it?' But no one in heaven or on earth or under the earth was able to open the scroll and read it. Then I began to weep ... But one of the twenty-four elders said to me, 'Stop weeping! Look, the Lion of the tribe of Judah, the heir to David's throne, has won the victory. He is worthy to open the scroll'* (from Revelation 5:1-5).

But when John looks for the Lion, instead he sees a Lamb, looking *as if it had been slaughtered, but it was now standing between the throne and the four living beings and among the twenty-four elders* (Revelation 5:6a). *Between* is a hugely important word here. While the Lamb of God stands *among the twenty-four elders*, He also stands *between* them and *the throne.*

Christ, who died for all the redeemed, the One True Church (represented by the 24 elders), is our go-between, our Advocate, the one who speaks on our behalf to the Father and says: "This one is mine." We are seen through the shed blood of Jesus and declared righteous because of his sacrifice. As Isaiah 61:10b declares, the Lord *has dressed* [us] *with the clothing of salvation and draped* [us] *in a robe of righteousness.*

John's description of the Lamb of God continues: *He had seven horns and seven eyes, which represent the sevenfold Spirit of God that is sent out into every part of the earth* (Revelation 5:6b).

[H]orns signify power, and *eyes* signify understanding or wisdom. John sees the Lamb of God with seven of each, meaning absolute, perfect power and wisdom. And John explains that these *horns and ... eyes ... represent the sevenfold Spirit of God that is sent out into every part of the earth.* All power, all wisdom belong to Christ, and he is God. He is the Holy Spirit. He is the Triune (three-in-one) God.

The Holy Spirit is not an "it." The Holy Spirit is God. It is no more appropriate to call the Holy Spirit "it" than it is to call Jesus Christ "it." If we believe in the Three-in-One Godhead—Father, Son, and Holy Spirit—it's important to acknowledge that the Holy Spirit is a manifestation equal to Christ himself, just as Christ is an equal manifestation of God himself.

When Jesus Christ left this Earth in his physical form, he remained with us in the form of the Holy Spirit. Long before Jesus' birth, Isaiah 7:14b foretold it: *The virgin will conceive a child! She will give birth to a son and will call him Immanuel (which means 'God is with us').*

God is still with us. The Holy Spirit lives inside every person who has truly committed their heart and life to Jesus Christ. He is calling to those who haven't already accepted Jesus Christ as Lord and Savior. He is with us. Not "it." He.

Thank him for his presence. Acknowledging his equality with God the Father and God the Son is a vital step toward a deeper understanding and walk with the Spirit.

Day 46

------------------------------------✦------------------------------------

We've seen that only Jesus Christ, the Lion of Judah, the Lamb of God, *is worthy to open the scroll* (from Revelation 5:5b).

And he came and took the scroll from the right hand of the one seated on the throne (Revelation 5:7). Stay with me here, but Jesus on the throne signifies His equality with God the Father. Jesus the Lamb shows him as the God-Man who gave his life as a living sacrifice for our sins. And the seven eyes of the Lamb *represent the sevenfold Spirit of God*, the Holy Spirit (Revelation 5:6b). The Holy Trinity is seen in this passage. I hope that helps clear up this confusing imagery a bit.

So Jesus takes *the scroll*, and all heaven breaks forth in celebration! We sometimes say, "Seems like I've waited an eternity for …" Heaven has been waiting that long.

When he had taken the scroll, the four living creatures and the twenty-four elders fell down before the Lamb. Each one had a harp, and they were holding golden bowls full of incense, which are the prayers of the saints. And they sang a new song: 'Worthy are you to take the scroll and open its seals, because you were slain, and by your blood you purchased for God those from every tribe and tongue and people and nation. You have made them into a kingdom, priests to serve our God, and they will reign upon the earth' (Revelation 5:8-10).

This is the passage that probably started the notion that every person who dies becomes an angel and flies around heaven plucking a harp. Let me knock this myth out of the way right quick. Angels are created beings, just as humans are created beings. Humans, however, are the only part of God's creation made in his own image. Speaking as the Trinity, we read God's words from Genesis 1:26a, *Let us make human beings in our image, to be like us.*

Angels, also created beings, have been around a lot longer than mankind. How do we know this? God says so in the Book of Job: *[W]hen I laid the foundations of the earth ... all the angels shouted for joy* (from Job 38:4, 7). And Psalm 103:21 speaks of the *armies of angels who serve Him and do His will!* Angels are servants of God. No human becomes an angel in heaven. And I assure you there's a whole lot more going on in heaven than harp-playing.

Lastly, let me also remind you that Lucifer, or Satan, was also an angel. As we saw a few days ago, he was actually one of the cherubim, or as Ezekiel 28:14 describes him, *an anointed guardian cherub* (ESV).

Lucifer not only turned against the Lord, he led other angels to follow him in his rebellion against their Creator. Some nerve, huh? And because of their sin, they were cast out of heaven forever.

But wait a minute. Every time we disobey the Lord through ignoring his will or choosing to go against it, we too are rebelling against our Creator. For the fallen angels, there was no going back. But praise God, for us there's grace! Forgiveness. Mercy. Aren't you thankful?

"Without grace there is no hope, but with it there is no shortage."—Christian author Barnabas Piper.

Day 47

Heaven is celebrating: *When he had taken the scroll, the four living creatures and the twenty-four elders fell down before the Lamb. Each one had a harp, and they were holding golden bowls full of incense, which are the prayers of the saints. And they sang a new song: 'Worthy are you to take the scroll and open its seals, because you were slain, and by your blood you purchased for God those from every tribe and tongue and people and nation. You have made them into a kingdom, priests to serve our God, and they will reign upon the earth'* (Revelation 5:8-10).

We're only hitting the highlights because it would take ages to cover all this in-depth, but for now, take a look at the *golden bowls full of incense, which are the prayers of the saints.*

If we look back at Luke 1, we see Zechariah serving as priest. Verse 10 says: *While the incense was being burned, a great crowd stood outside, praying.* Ezra 6:10 speaks of *offering incense to the God of heaven and ... praying* (NET).

In heaven, no believer is *outside* as the prayers of God's people are being lifted up. The One True Church is in the very presence of God.

And they sang a new song. Commentary on this one statement could fill volumes, but here are some important points:

(1) Why is the song *new*? For the saints of the Old Testament, their long-awaited Deliverer had come.

(2) It was *new* to be sealed with the Holy Spirit. Paul explains in Ephesians 1:13: *And in him, having heard and believed the word of truth—the gospel of your salvation—you were sealed with the promised Holy Spirit* (BSB).

(3) It was *new* to be *a royal priesthood ... God's special possession* (I Peter 2:9, NIV), *priests to serve our God, and ... reign upon the earth* (Revelation 5:10).

And all this was possible because of Jesus' great sacrifice. His *blood ... purchased for God those from every tribe and tongue and people and nation* (Revelation 5:9b). Who is the *those* this passage speaks of? Jesus, referring to himself as *the gate*, said in John 10:9, *Those who come in through me will be saved.*

Is there only one way? In these last days, I'm hearing many people ask that question. A greater number of people are beginning to think there are multiple ways to heaven. Let me put it plainly: there aren't. Speaking of Jesus in Acts 4:12, Peter declared: *There is salvation in no one else! God has given no other name under heaven by which we must be saved.*

If you don't know Jesus, you'll never know heaven. If your friends and family don't know Jesus, they'll never know heaven. Time is short. Make sure you get the Word out.

Day 48

Jesus, the Lamb of God, was the only one worthy to take the scroll John saw in heaven. ***And when he took the scroll, the four living beings and the twenty-four elders fell down before the Lamb ... And they sang a new song*** (Revelation 5:8a, 9a).

The celebration began. What a monumental occasion this is! The One True Church is in heaven. Jesus is about to open the scroll and the final days before his Millennial Reign are about to begin:

Then I looked again, and I heard the voices of thousands and millions of angels around the throne and of the living beings and the elders. And they sang in a mighty chorus: 'Worthy is the Lamb who was slaughtered—to receive power and riches and wisdom and strength and honor and glory and blessing' (Revelation 5:11-12).

There's no way to even begin to take in this scene. John is describing the indescribable in the best human terms possible. He sees and hears ***the four living beings and the twenty-four elders*** along with ***thousands and millions of angels*** singing praises to the Lamb. The Bible recounts many times when the appearance of one angel struck a person speechless in terror and awe. There's no way to conceive the sight of ***thousands and millions***.

And the party was only getting started. It expanded throughout the heavens and even onto the Earth: ***And then I heard every creature in heaven and on earth and under the earth and in the sea. They sang: 'Blessing and honor and glory and power belong to the one sitting on the throne and to the Lamb forever and ever'*** (Revelation 5:13).

Psalm 96:13a declares: ***Let all creation rejoice before the Lord*** (NIV).

And as ***every creature in heaven and on earth and under the earth and in the sea*** joined the celebration, ***the four living beings said, 'Amen!' And the twenty-four elders fell down and worshiped the Lamb*** (Revelation 5:14).

Amen! In other words, so be it! Yes, a million times over! This is the moment ***all creation*** has been waiting for. And if you're a part of the One True Church, you're going to be right there joining in this incredible celebration. Don't you dare miss it.

Revelation 6

Day 49

Yesterday we saw the huge celebration that began in heaven and spread to *every creature in heaven and on earth and under the earth and in the sea* (Revelation 5:13a). The Lamb of God had been declared worthy to open the scroll. That scroll, as we saw a while back, was sealed with seven seals. Now Jesus begins to open those seals.

As I watched, the Lamb broke the first of the seven seals on the scroll. Then I heard one of the four living beings say with a voice like thunder, 'Come!' I looked up and saw a white horse standing there. Its rider carried a bow, and a crown was placed on his head. He rode out to win many battles and gain the victory (Revelation 6:1-2).

We're wading into some deep waters here, so let me stress that there are differing opinions on the identity of the rider of this first white horse. Some believe him to be Jesus. Others believe him to be the Antichrist. I agree with the latter. Yes, we will see Jesus on a white horse later on—see Revelation 19—but this isn't him. Why don't I believe this is Jesus?

First, Jesus is the one opening the seal. Second, I don't see even one of the cherubim—*the four living beings*—ordering Jesus to *Come!* or to do anything else. Third, this figure rides *out to win many battles and gain the victory.* Jesus doesn't need to *gain the victory*. It's already his.

Fourth, once the Church is removed from the world, the time will have come for the Antichrist to have his brief period of power. This is when he will appear as the false messiah. My fifth and final point is what follows this white horse and its rider: three more riders, none of whom bring anything good.

When the Lamb opened the second seal, I heard the second living creature say, 'Come!' Then another horse came out, a fiery red one. Its rider was given power to take peace from the earth and to make people kill each other. To him was given a large sword (Revelation 6:3-4, NIV).

If there was any doubt about the identity of the first rider, the riders who follow him should remove it. The red horse and its rider have one mission: *to take peace from the earth and to make people kill each other.*

With the Church removed from the Earth, God's judgment has begun. The Antichrist is given temporary authority on Earth. The red horse and its rider represent war, but he is only able *to take peace from the earth* because he *was given power to* do so. Who gave him that power? God. The Holy Trinity. God has given the Earth every opportunity to repent and turn to him. Now, with those who are his own out of danger, the end-time horrors have begun.

You've heard it said so many times, but it can't be said enough: Jesus is going to call his people out from this Earth, and those who haven't committed their hearts and lives to him will be left behind to endure the horrors of the Tribulation. I wouldn't wish that on anyone. Nor should you.

Make sure you're ready to go, and make sure you're helping others prepare.

Day 50

Jesus has begun to open the seven seals on the scroll. Opening the first seal unleashed a white horse and rider who looked like Jesus but was actually the Antichrist. Satan is an imposter.

The opening of the second seal brings out a red horse and rider, War. As I said yesterday, with the Church removed from the Earth, God's judgment has begun. The Lord has given the Earth every opportunity to repent and turn to him. Now, with those who are his own having been taken up into heaven, the end-time terrors have begun.

When the Lamb opened the third seal, I heard the third living creature say, 'Come!' I looked, and there before me was a black horse! Its rider was holding a pair of scales in his hand. Then I heard what sounded like a voice among the four living creatures, saying, 'Two pounds of wheat for a day's wages, and six pounds of barley for a day's wages, and do not damage the oil and the wine!' (Revelation 6:5-6, NIV).

The black horse and its rider represent Famine. This rider's purpose is to destroy the food supplies on Earth. As food becomes more and more scarce, the prices increase until enough wheat or barley to barely keep a family alive for a few days costs a day's wages.

[D]o not damage the oil and the wine! There are a couple of viewpoints on this. First, the wealthy will still be able to afford these, even though they're luxury items. The second train of thought is that these items will still be available, but who can live on only oil and wine? Oil was used in cooking and a weak low-alcohol content wine was commonly drunk with meals. Bottom

101

line, though, is that Famine will strike the entire Earth and starvation will be rampant.

Next, Jesus opens the fourth seal and the last of the four horsemen makes his appearance. *When the Lamb opened the fourth seal, I heard the voice of the fourth living creature say, 'Come!' I looked, and there before me was a pale horse! Its rider was named Death, and Hades was following close behind him. They were given power over a fourth of the earth to kill by sword, famine and plague, and by the wild beasts of the earth* (Revelation 6:7-8, NIV).

The pale horse's rider is immediately identified: Death. With the Antichrist in power, and war and famine happening all over the world, bodies are piling up and disease (*plague*) is everywhere. Many of the dead and dying are devoured *by the wild beasts of the earth*. Next comes Hades, hell. The unsaved of Earth leave earthly horror only to be swallowed up in eternal damnation.

We've seen all four of the horsemen and riders now, but there are three more seals to be opened. How we need to take to heart the advance warning John was allowed to give. This horrible, dreadful time is inescapable for those who aren't taken up to heaven in the Rapture.

Talk to your family. Talk to your friends. Use every opportunity you have to speak about the end times. Make sure people understand the urgency to commit their lives to Jesus.

Day 51

Jesus has opened the first four seals on the scroll and we've seen all four of the horsemen and riders, but there are three more seals to be opened.

When the Lamb broke the fifth seal, I saw under the altar the souls of all who had been martyred for the word of God and for being faithful in their testimony. They shouted to the Lord and said, 'O Sovereign Lord, holy and true, how long before you judge the people who belong to this world and avenge our blood for what they have done to us?' Then a white robe was given to each of them. And they were told to rest a little longer until the full number of their brothers and sisters—their fellow servants of Jesus who were to be martyred—had joined them (Revelation 6:9-11).

There are two different opinions as to the identity of these *souls ... under the altar*. One view is that these are all the martyrs from all time. The other—and this is where I throw my hat in—see these as people who were saved on Earth after the Rapture of the Church (during the Tribulation) and were killed because of their faithfulness and testimony to others.

Why are they *under the altar*? This was an understandable visual for John. Like the blood of the sacrifices in the Temple, these Tribulation saints had spilled their blood rather than deny the one they'd finally come to believe in.

These martyrs cried out to the Lord, *O Sovereign Lord, holy and true, how long before you judge the people who belong to this world and avenge our blood for what they have done to us?* This wasn't simply a cry of "Look what they did to us." This is a cry for the Tribulation to be over and for the horrors to end. Undoubtedly, these *souls* weren't the only ones saved during the Tribulation. They knew there were others who had become part of the family of God, their brothers and sisters in Christ, who were enduring unthinkable torment at the hands of the Antichrist and his followers.

This is further verified by the instructions they were given to *rest a little longer until the full number of their brothers and sisters—their fellow servants of Jesus who were to be martyred—had joined them.*

Many people will put their faith in Jesus during the Tribulation, but they will pay a great price for having waited until that time. As 2 Corinthians 6:2b reminds us: *Today is the day of salvation.* Sadly, though, countless people won't be saved when the Church is taken into heaven, and those who aren't will be left behind to endure the reign of the Antichrist.

For those who turn to Jesus even during those last days, their reward is heaven. But what a terrible way to get there. Don't wait to commit your heart and life to Jesus. And don't wait to tell others how much they need him.

Day 52

I watched as the Lamb broke the sixth seal, and there was a great earthquake. The sun became as dark as black cloth, and the moon became as red as blood. Then the stars of the sky fell to the earth like green figs falling from a tree shaken by a strong wind. The sky was rolled up like a scroll, and all of the mountains and islands were moved from their places.

Then everyone—the kings of the earth, the rulers, the generals, the wealthy, the powerful, and every slave and free person—all hid themselves in the caves and among the rocks of the mountains. And they cried to the mountains and the rocks, 'Fall on us and hide us from the face of the one who sits on the throne and from the wrath of the Lamb. For the great day of their wrath has come, and who is able to survive?' (Revelation 6:12-17).

The opening of the sixth seal throws the universe into utter chaos. An earthquake rocks the entire planet. The sun stops shining and the moon looks like blood. The stars—monster-sized meteorites—fall to the Earth. The sky seems to disappear and whole mountains are leveled even as islands sink beneath the ocean. Earth is doomed, and all those who haven't given their hearts and lives to Jesus are doomed right along with it.

John's depiction of what's happening isn't symbolic. It's real. It's his best possible description of a cataclysmic event like no one has ever seen. Thank God, the Church won't be here when it happens!

With the internet and all sorts of instant communication worldwide, reports would be coming in from everywhere about these awful disasters. And then the lights go out. The satellites, like the sun, moon, and stars, go dark. No one knows what's happening anywhere except right where they are, and all they see around them is absolute horror.

No wonder John says *everyone—the kings of the earth, the rulers, the generals, the wealthy, the powerful, and every slave and free person* cried out, begging for the rocks to fall on them. Never has there been the kind of terror the people left on Earth will experience during this time.

And out of all these horrors, what is it the people will fear the most? *[T]he face of the one who sits on the throne and ... the wrath of the Lamb.* Too late now for repentance. Too late now for anything except the present and eternal suffering that awaits those who have rejected Jesus' free offer of salvation.

And all this happens with every person fully aware of why it's happening: Because *the great day of* [the Lord's] *wrath has come.*

This is reality. And it's a reality that every person living on Planet Earth will experience during the last days. Only the redeemed will escape. Only the redeemed will have already been scooped up and taken to the eternal safety of the Father's arms.

Live like you believe this so that others will believe it too.

Revelation 7

Day 53

Jesus has opened the sixth seal, and its opening throws the universe into chaos. An earthquake rocks the entire planet. The sun stops shining and the moon looks like blood. The stars fall to the Earth. The sky vanishes, mountains collapse, and islands sink beneath the ocean. Earth is doomed, and all those who haven't given their hearts and lives to Jesus are doomed right along with it.

Even as everyone cries out, begging for the rocks to fall on them, they do so because of their terror of *the face of the one who sits on the throne and... the wrath of the Lamb* (Revelation 6:16b). At this point, there are no atheists left on Earth. Every person knows who's in charge and why all this is happening. Too late, they now realize that every word in the Bible is true.

Then I saw four angels standing at the four corners of the earth, holding back the four winds so they did not blow on the earth or the sea, or even on any tree. And I saw another angel coming up from the east, carrying the seal of the living God. And he shouted to those four angels, who had been given power to harm land and sea, 'Wait! Don't harm the land or the sea or the trees until we have placed the seal of God on the foreheads of His servants.' And I heard how many were marked with the seal of God—144,000 were sealed from all the tribes of Israel: from Judah, 12,000; from Reuben, 12,000; from Gad, 12,000; from

Asher, 12,000; from Naphtali, 12,000; from Manasseh, 12,000; from Simeon, 12,000; from Levi, 12,000; from Issachar, 12,000; from Zebulun, 12,000; from Joseph, 12,000; from Benjamin, 12,000 (Revelation 7:1-8).

We're wading in deep again, but this seems to be an event prior to the unleashing of the four horsemen, as *the four winds* are likely to represent the same four horsemen. The catastrophes taking place on Earth are held off until 144,000 special witnesses are sealed*: [U]ntil we have placed the seal of God on the foreheads of His servants.*

Who are these 144,000 special witnesses? Jews. Jews who have believed on Jesus Christ as the Messiah. Jews who have a special assignment from God. What is it? We aren't told any specifics, but they are assuredly telling the world that Jesus is God. Who knows how many of the martyred souls we saw in yesterday's passage came to Christ through these people's testimonies.

Records showing who came from which tribe are long gone, but God knows everything about everyone, and these 144,000 are made up of 12,000 from each of the listed tribes. But there's something very interesting in this list: (1) the tribe of Dan isn't listed; and (2) Joseph is listed, even though Joseph is actually the tribes of Ephraim and Manasseh. If you look back at the list, Manasseh has its own listing, but Ephraim doesn't. So Joseph must be the listing for the tribe of Ephraim. I hope that makes sense.

To clarify before I wrap up for today, contrary to what some have been taught, there will assuredly be more than 144,000 people saved and going to heaven. Nobody has to beat out another person to get a spot in glory. Besides, since our right standing before the Lord is only because of the sacrifice of Christ, my standing before him is just as solid as Billy Graham's. And so is yours. Incredible, yes, but that's the amazing God we've put our trust in.

We'll take a deeper look at these 144,000 tomorrow.

Day 54

After the opening of the sixth seal in Chapter 6, we came to Chapter 7 where we did a quick review to see that none of the four horsemen were allowed to begin their campaigns of chaos until the designated angels had *placed the seal of God on the foreheads of His servants* (Revelation 7:3b).

While all the redeemed are sealed with the Holy Spirit (see Ephesians 1:13), these 144,000 special servants are all Jews, from what appears to be 11 of the 12 tribes of Israel. As I said yesterday, there is no mention of Dan in this list. Why would Dan be left out? We can only speculate, but it could be because that was the first tribe to bring the practice of idolatry into Israel: *Then they set up the carved image* (Judges 18:30a).

But don't count Dan out. Just because they aren't mentioned in Revelation's 144,000 as special witnesses for the Lord doesn't mean the descendants of Dan are without hope. In Ezekiel's great vision (see Ezekiel 40-48), Dan is the first tribe mentioned after Ezekiel describes the river of healing flowing from the Temple of the Holy City (see Ezekiel 48:1). God's forgiveness is beyond our comprehension. Before we count anybody out, we need to remember that.

Speaking of not counting people out, let's see what John saw next in heaven: *After this I saw a vast crowd, too great to count, from every nation and tribe and people and language, standing in front of the throne and before the Lamb. They were clothed in white robes and held palm branches in their hands. And they were shouting with a great roar, 'Salvation comes from our God who sits on the throne and from the Lamb!'* (Revelation 7:9-10).

Here's a brand new crowd, *a vast crowd, too great to count, from every nation and tribe and people and language*, added to the enormous celebration going on all over creation. And who else was worshiping? *[A]ll the angels were standing around the throne and around the elders and the four living beings. And they fell before the throne with their faces to the ground and worshiped God. They sang, 'Amen! Blessing and glory and wisdom and thanksgiving and honor and power and strength belong to our God forever and ever! Amen'* (Revelation 7:11-12).

Then one of the twenty-four elders asked me, 'Who are these who are clothed in white? Where did they come from?' And I said to him, 'Sir, you are the one who knows' (Revelation 7:13-14a).

None of us can begin to visualize what John was feeling as he witnessed this scene and the many other wonders of heaven. But it's important to realize that eternity is timeless, so what John sees isn't necessarily in chronological order as we understand time. Now one of the elders tells John who this *vast crowd* is: *Then he said to me, 'These are the ones who died in the great tribulation. They have washed their robes in the blood of the Lamb and made them white'* (Revelation 7:14b).

As horrible as the Tribulation will be, this will be a time when countless people will turn to Jesus. Finally, in the midst of horrors this world has never seen before nor will ever see again, droves of people will figure out the Bible was telling the Absolute Truth from cover to cover.

As I said before, there won't be an atheist left on Planet Earth. I pray everyone reading this is a committed believer. It grieves me beyond words to think of anyone being left behind to endure the Tribulation. But even for those who are, don't count them out. God's forgiveness is so much deeper and wider than anything we can even begin to imagine.

Day 55

John saw *a vast crowd, too great to count, from every nation and tribe and people and language, standing in front of the throne and before the Lamb. They were clothed in white robes and held palm branches in their hands. And they were shouting with a great roar, 'Salvation comes from our God who sits on the throne and from the Lamb!'* (Revelation 7:9-10).

This is not the huge crowd John saw earlier. This is the group we saw for the first time yesterday. Who are they? *These are the ones who died in the great tribulation. They have washed their robes in the blood of the Lamb and made them white* (Revelation 7:14b). During the horrors of the Tribulation, countless people will put their faith in Jesus.

And as more and more people realize the truth of the Bible and turn to Jesus, they'll tell others who'll tell others—just like we're to be doing now but with far more urgency than most Christians today. Too, there'll be the witness of the 144,000 Jewish believers who'll have accepted Christ and will have special protection during the Tribulation, *the seal of God on the foreheads of His servants* (Revelation 7:3b).

The elder who identified the *vast crowd* for John now tells John why their jubilation is so effusive. They knew what terrors their salvation had rescued them from. If ever there was a time that could be described as hell on earth, the Tribulation comes as close as that will ever get. Even though these believers had suffered horribly and been killed for their faith in Christ, they understood the eternal horror they'd been saved from, and they understood the great price paid for their salvation.

That is why they stand in front of God's throne and serve him day and night in his Temple. And he who sits on the throne will give them shelter. They will never again be hungry or thirsty; they will never be scorched by the heat of the sun. For the Lamb on the throne will be their Shepherd. He will lead them to springs of life-giving water. And God will wipe every tear from their eyes (Revelation 7:15-17).

Look back at the above passage. Based on what the elder tells John, we can surmise that these believers who were saved during the Tribulation endured many hardships, including having no shelter, no food, and no water. In other words, they had nothing. The very basics of life had been denied them because of their commitment to Christ.

Now, though, these saints of God had no needs whatsoever. God himself provided them with an eternal home; a seat at the banquet table of Christ; *life-giving water*; and a joyful eternity where none of them would ever shed another tear.

Why is it we most deeply appreciate the good things in our lives only after we've been through bad things? Whether you've had a life of ease or experienced a lot of hardships and heartaches, knowing Jesus Christ as Lord and Savior guarantees you eternity with *no more death or sorrow or crying or pain* (Revelation 21:4b).

Sounds wonderful, doesn't it? And if it sounds wonderful to you, it'll sound just as wonderful to the people with whom you share the Good News.

Revelation 8

Day 56

The Tribulation saints have been gathered into heaven. And now Jesus opens the seventh seal on the scroll: *When the Lamb broke the seventh seal on the scroll, there was silence throughout heaven for about half an hour* (Revelation 8:1).

All creation had been shouting and praising Jesus. Now there comes a time of absolute silence. John says *for about half an hour*. What a contrast! And what does this mean?

In a place where loud sounds of worship are nonstop, this has to be a deafening silence. Have you ever been in a meeting when the speaker loses his place and there's that awkward moment of hesitation or silence? In a matter of seconds, the whole room feels the discomfort.

Perhaps that's what's going on in heaven here. With the final seal removed, the scroll can now be opened and the judgments begun. This is the moment all creation has been waiting for: the beginning of the end, when Christ will make all things right.

After the seventh seal is opened, John says, *I saw the seven angels who stand before God, and they were given seven trumpets* (Revelation 8:2). Jewish tradition even says there are seven angels who stand in God's presence. And here we see them, and they've been given seven trumpets because the time has come to sound the battle cry. With each trumpet blast, a judgment begins.

But even before that, some other things happen in heaven and on Earth: *Then another angel with a gold incense burner came and stood at the altar. And a great amount of incense was given to him to mix with the prayers of God's people as an offering on the gold altar before the throne. The smoke of the incense, mixed with the prayers of God's holy people, ascended up to God from the altar where the angel had poured them out. Then the angel filled the incense burner with fire from the altar and threw it down upon the earth; and thunder crashed, lightning flashed, and there was a terrible earthquake* (Revelation 8:3-4).

Like the incense offered to the Lord in the Temple, this angel blends heavenly incense with *the prayers of God's people*. Just a thought here, but, figuratively, this incense may represent the actions of Christ as *a sacrifice for us, a pleasing aroma to God* (Ephesians 5:2b). As our *High Priest* (Hebrews 8:3), Jesus brings the prayers of the saints before the Father.

The incense having been poured out, the angel's mission now changed. *The angel filled the incense burner with fire from the altar and threw it down upon the earth; and thunder crashed, lightning flashed, and there was a terrible earthquake* (Revelation 8:5).

As I've said before, time isn't necessarily chronological in Revelation, so each of the seven trumpets seem to coincide with the opening of each of the seven seals. Tomorrow we'll start our look at what each trumpet brings.

Day 57

The Lamb of God has opened all seven seals on the scroll he was holding, and after an explosion of praise, there came *silence throughout heaven for about half an hour* (Revelation 8:1). After this, John *saw the seven angels who stand before God, and they were given seven trumpets* (Revelation 8:2).

Before the seven angels with trumpets, *another angel with a gold incense burner* is seen (Revelation 8:3). He mixed the incense with the prayers of God's people which then *ascended up to God from the altar where the angel had poured them out* (Revelation 8:4). This same angel then *filled the incense burner with fire from the altar and threw it down upon the earth; and thunder crashed, lightning flashed, and there was a terrible earthquake* (Revelation 8:5).

Then the seven angels with the seven trumpets prepared to blow their mighty blasts (Revelation 8:6). Once again, let me remind you that the occurrences in the Book of Revelation are not necessarily in chronological order. These seven angels blowing their trumpets may or may not coincide with the opening of each of the seven seals, but at whatever point these trumpets are blown, each one brings more of God's judgment upon the earth.

The first angel blew his trumpet, and hail and fire mixed with blood were thrown down on the earth. One-third of the earth was set on fire, one-third of the trees were burned, and all the green grass was burned (Revelation 8:7).

Whatever brings about the *hail and fire mixed with blood* described by John, we can't be sure, but it takes out one-third of the plants on Earth. Speculation runs the gamut from a gigantic meteorite to nuclear warfare. There are countless possible explanations. The important thing, though, is to: (A) plan on not being here when this happens; and (B) understand that however it takes place, this is God bringing judgment on a world that has rejected its own Creator.

Then the second angel blew his trumpet, and a great mountain of fire was thrown into the sea. One-third of the water in the sea became blood, one-third of all things living in the sea died, and one-third of all the ships on the sea were destroyed (Revelation 8:8-9).

The Creator is turning his creation against those who have rejected him. Whether this *great mountain of fire* that falls *into the sea* is another meteorite or some other horrifying phenomenon, it destroys *one-third of all things living in the sea ... and one-third of all the ships on the sea.*

And we've only looked at the first two trumpeters. Any way you want to explain or guess at what will be happening on Earth during this time, it's safe to say there is irreversible ecological and geological destruction on an unheard-of scale. And it will only get worse.

Everything we're reading about in Revelation is real. Every bit of this will take place after Jesus calls his Bride to be with him in glory. Every awful thing we read about will affect the people who are still here after the Church is taken up. Don't be left behind, and plead with others to make sure they won't be, either.

Day 58

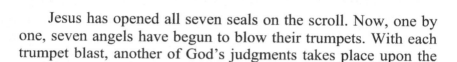

Jesus has opened all seven seals on the scroll. Now, one by one, seven angels have begun to blow their trumpets. With each trumpet blast, another of God's judgments takes place upon the earth.

The first angel blew his trumpet, and hail and fire mixed with blood were thrown down on the earth. One-third of the earth was set on fire, one-third of the trees were burned, and all the green grass was burned. Then the second angel blew his trumpet, and a great mountain of fire was thrown into the sea. One-third of the water in the sea became blood, one-third of all things living in the sea died, and one-third of all the ships on the sea were destroyed (Revelation 8:8-9).

Then the third angel blew his trumpet, and a great star fell from the sky, burning like a torch. It fell on one-third of the rivers and on the springs of water. The name of the star was Bitterness. It made one-third of the water bitter, and many people died from drinking the bitter water (Revelation 8:10-11).

This third trumpet blast brings about another horrible disaster, this time ruining one-third of the world's fresh waters. The **great star** may actually be a star or some other type of meteorite. As I said yesterday, whatever is happening is causing irreversible ecological and geological destruction. The water becomes so contaminated that people die from drinking it.

The star itself is called **Bitterness**, or in some translations "Wormwood," which is a very bitter herb. The word *wormwood* is used in Deuteronomy, Amos, Jeremiah, Lamentations, and Proverbs as a reference to sorrow and bitterness.

The world has never seen the sorrow and bitterness that awaits those who are left behind after those belonging to Jesus Christ are taken from this world. We've already seen one-third of the vegetation destroyed; one-third of the seas and everything in them destroyed, along with the ships, crews, and passengers on the sea; and one-third of the rivers, springs, and other fresh waters destroyed or contaminated to the point of being unable to sustain life for anything living in them or drinking from them.

We'll look at the fourth trumpet blast tomorrow. All I can say is: people, get ready, get ready.

Day 59

Now the fourth angel goes to work: *Then the fourth angel blew his trumpet, and one-third of the sun was struck, and one-third of the moon, and one-third of the stars, and they became dark. And one-third of the day was dark, and also one-third of the night* (Revelation 8:12).

This time, the sun itself is affected by whatever the Lord is orchestrating. With a one-third portion of all the celestial lights affected, Earth becomes a cold, dark, terrifying place. Night is, of course, darker than day, but what's happening now is a darkness as black as the darkest cave.

Add to that the destruction of the vegetation, seas, and fresh waters, and it's clearly a view of a crumbling planet filled with dying people. People who are not only dying physically, but also dying spiritually unless they turn to the only one who can save them.

Then I looked, and I heard a single eagle crying loudly as it flew through the air, 'Terror, terror, terror to all who belong to this world because of what will happen when the last three angels blow their trumpets' (Revelation 8:13).

Who is in terror? *[A]ll who belong to this world.* The Apostle Peter reminds us, *Dear friends, I warn you as 'temporary residents and foreigners' to keep away from worldly desires that wage war against your very souls* (1 Peter 2:11).

The Israelites spent hundreds of years as slaves in Egypt. Even after being miraculously delivered from that place, they chose time and again to disobey Jehovah. For generations, Egypt had been all they knew. This world is the only home we know.

119

And like the Israelites, we find it so easy to forget that we are only *temporary residents and foreigners*. We struggle daily *to keep away from worldly desires that wage war against* [our] *very souls.*

Yet what does Jesus tell us? *I am not of this world* (John 8:23b, NIV). *My kingdom is not of this world* (John 8:36a). And if you know Jesus as your Lord and Savior, this world is not your home, either.

In the great faith chapter of Hebrews 11, the writer reminds us that these saints of old *agreed that they were foreigners and nomads here on earth. But they were looking for a better place, a heavenly homeland. That is why God is not ashamed to be called their God, for he has prepared a city for them* (Hebrews 11:13b, 16).

Those *who belong to this world* end up with the same fate as *this world*. But for his own, God *has prepared a city*. Are you coming?

Day 60

The fourth angel has blown his trumpet and one-third of the sun, the stars, and the moon have gone dark. The universe is crumbling and, along with it, the people who have rejected Jesus Christ as Lord and Savior.

Then I looked, and I heard a single eagle crying loudly as it flew through the air, 'Terror, terror, terror to all who belong to this world because of what will happen when the last three angels blow their trumpets' (Revelation 8:13).

As we saw yesterday, the only people who have anything to fear from all these disasters are *all who belong to this world.* And don't miss what the eagle is crying: *Terror, terror, terror.* The number three is also a number symbolizing completeness, so this tells us that the terrors of these events are full force.

But note what else we see in the disasters brought on by the trumpet blasts of these first four angels: only one-third of the world is being devastated at this time. Even in the midst of such horrific judgment, we see God's mercy. One-third may be destroyed, but, for now, two-thirds are spared. There is still time for many to repent, if only they will.

But what specific terror does the eagle speak of? *[W]hat will happen when the last three angels blow their trumpets.* If you think what we're reading about now is terrifying, there's even worse to come.

Then the fifth angel blew his trumpet, and I saw a star that had fallen to earth from the sky, and he was given the key to the shaft of the bottomless pit. When he opened it, smoke poured out as though from a huge furnace, and the sunlight and air turned dark from the smoke (Revelation 9:1-2).

The *star* referred to in this passage is clearly not an actual star, but a person or being because the same passage says *he was given the key to the shaft of the bottomless pit.* No, this is not Satan. Satan isn't in charge and the Lord is certainly not going to give him *the key to the shaft of the bottomless pit.* But whether this is an actual fallen angel—a demon—or a heavenly angel, God is in charge, and he is the one who has given this being the authority to unlock the pit.

And when the pit is opened, so much smoke and, undoubtedly, fire and heat, pour out that *the sunlight and air turned dark.* No horror movie can compare with what's about to come out of that pit.

All those who know Jesus as Lord and Savior leave this world and enter into glory. If we'll remember that, we'll have no fear for ourselves, but a tremendous urgency to warn those who don't know him.

Revelation 9

Day 61

This is what we covered yesterday: ***Then the fifth angel blew his trumpet, and I saw a star that had fallen to earth from the sky, and he was given the key to the shaft of the bottomless pit. When he opened it, smoke poured out as though from a huge furnace, and the sunlight and air turned dark from the smoke*** (Revelation 9:1-2).

What happened next? ***Then locusts came from the smoke and descended on the earth, and they were given power to sting like scorpions. They were told not to harm the grass or plants or trees, but only the people who did not have the seal of God on their foreheads. They were told not to kill them but to torture them for five months with pain like the pain of a scorpion sting. In those days people will seek death but will not find it. They will long to die, but death will flee from them!*** (Revelation 9:3-6).

These so-called ***locusts*** aren't locusts at all, but demons being released onto the Earth. While Satan has had some power on Earth all along, with the Church no longer here, he is allowed to have far more power. Temporarily. The demons are ***given power to sting like scorpions***. Whether these stings are literal or figurative, we can be certain that these demons will be sent out to inflict maximum pain by some means on the people remaining on Earth.

However, certain people are off limits: *They were told not to harm ... the people who ... have the seal of God on their foreheads.* And the only people with *the seal of God on their foreheads* are the 144,000 special Jewish witnesses (see Revelation 7:3-4).

As for the rest of the people remaining on Earth, *They were told not to kill them but to torture them for five months with pain like the pain of a scorpion sting.* I'm only speculating here, but it is possible that even though the 144,000 are turning many people to faith in Jesus Christ, the people who repent and turn to Jesus are quickly martyred for their faith. Only the 144,000 *who ... have the seal of God on their foreheads* have a special protection over them that enables them to survive throughout the Tribulation. Remember, this special group was saved after the Church was taken from Earth and remain on Earth as witnesses to lead others to Jesus.

In those days people will seek death but will not find it. They will long to die, but death will flee from them! While God has allowed this demonic attack, he is also limiting it to *five months*. Even in his righteous judgments, God shows great mercy.

Note, too, that other than the 144,000 who are specially protected, the people of Earth *will seek death but will not find it*. Is God taking pleasure in their suffering? No. As with all the other horrors of the Tribulation, he is using evil to give those who don't know him a clear choice to repent and be saved.

If the people of Earth during this time were able to die from these demonic attacks, they would die forever condemned because of their unbelief. But not allowing these attacks to be fatal means that every living person remaining on Earth will have more opportunities to turn to Jesus.

Even as we see such great horror, we see even greater mercy. The people who have rejected the Lord time and again are still not without hope. Jesus Christ will still receive any person who turns to him in repentance and faith. I pray everyone reading this has already made that commitment.

Day 62

Yesterday we saw that these demonic spirits from the bottomless pit John described as *locusts came from the smoke ... and were given power to sting like scorpions* (Revelation 9:3). Even though their stings will be incredibly painful, the people who are stung won't die. Why? Because even in this judgment, God's mercy will allow these people yet another opportunity to repent and believe in Jesus.

John continues his description: *The locusts looked like horses prepared for battle. They had what looked like gold crowns on their heads, and their faces looked like human faces. They had hair like women's hair and teeth like the teeth of a lion. They wore armor made of iron, and their wings roared like an army of chariots rushing into battle. They had tails that stung like scorpions, and for five months they had the power to torment people. Their king is the angel from the bottomless pit; his name in Hebrew is Abaddon, and in Greek, Apollyon—the Destroyer* (Revelation 9:7-11).

I've heard all sorts of speculation about what is being described here. Some think the *human faces* are literal and the *gold crowns* are helmets worn by the occupants of helicopters or some other type of modern-day warcraft with *wings* [that] *roared like an army of chariots*. Maybe, maybe not. Whatever these are, they're demonic and led by Satan himself, also referred to as *Abaddon, Apollyon*, and *the Destroyer*.

Think for a moment about this. Satan as the Destroyer has one goal: to destroy the lives of everyone he can, not just temporarily but for eternity. He knows he's fighting a battle he's already lost, so his only pleasure is in taking with him as many humans—the only part of creation made in the very image of God (see Genesis 1:27)—as he possibly can.

With God's protection in place, Satan is allowed to inflict tremendous suffering, but he isn't allowed to kill. And only by the death of a person who doesn't know Jesus as Lord and Savior does Satan find his greatest satisfaction. It isn't enough to cause a person to suffer on this Earth. He wants human beings to join him in his eternal fate *in the eternal fire* Jesus warns us about in Matthew 25:41.

Imagine the anger and frustration of this demonic leader when everything he does still doesn't result in death for these people. This is why John warns us that what he's described is bad, but there's still worse to come: ***The first terror is past, but look, two more terrors are coming!*** (Revelation 9:12).

If you know Jesus, get busy telling others what's coming. Share this study with people who want to know or understand more about the message in the Book of Revelation. And pray, pray, pray for the Holy Spirit to speak to the hearts of those who aren't prepared for the day when Jesus Christ calls his Bride, the Church, into glory.

Day 63

Then the sixth angel blew his trumpet, and I heard a voice speaking from the four horns of the gold altar that stands in the presence of God. And the voice said to the sixth angel who held the trumpet, 'Release the four angels who are bound at the great Euphrates River.' Then the four angels who had been prepared for this hour and day and month and year were turned loose to kill one-third of all the people on earth. I heard the size of their army, which was 200 million mounted troops (Revelation 9:13-16).

The four horns of the gold altar. (1) This was the altar where incense was offered to the Lord and, as we read in Chapter 8, the prayers of God's people are mingled with the incense and offered up to God. It is impossible to stress strongly enough the power of the prayers of God's people. (2) The blood of the sacrifice was placed on the four horns of the altar. The sacrifice of Christ on the cross paid the sin-debt for all who put their faith in Him. But Psalm 116:17 also speaks of the *sacrifice of thanksgiving*, which may also be alluded to here.

How can it be a sacrifice to praise the Lord? Years ago, I was listening to a broadcast of "Focus on the Family" and a woman was talking about her and her husband's experience when they lost eight of their nine children in a terrible accident. She and her husband were both badly injured and, as the EMTs loaded her onto the stretcher, she kept quoting Job 13:15: *Though he slay me, yet will I trust in him* (KJV).

One of the paramedics turned to another one and said, "She's delirious."

127

She immediately responded, "No, I'm not. I just know if I don't praise him now, I may never praise him again." In times of overwhelming sorrow, praise is indeed sacrifice.

For those who turn to Jesus during the Tribulation, things will be dreadful, but as they offer their sacrifices of praise, he will sustain them until they are martyred and join him in glory.

If you're going through a rough patch, praise him now. If you'll let him, I promise he'll wrap you in his arms of love and lift your spirits far above your situation.

Day 64

Then the sixth angel blew his trumpet, and I heard a voice speaking from the four horns of the gold altar that stands in the presence of God. And the voice said to the sixth angel who held the trumpet, 'Release the four angels who are bound at the great Euphrates River.' Then the four angels who had been prepared for this hour and day and month and year were turned loose to kill one-third of all the people on earth. I heard the size of their army, which was 200 million mounted troops (Revelation 9:13-16).

Who are these four angels? We aren't told, so we can only speculate. They could be the same four angels mentioned in Chapter 7, but I don't think so. After all, these four angels are said to be **bound**. A holy angel wouldn't be chained or held back, so it's a safe assumption that these four angels are demonic forces that have been restrained until this very moment.

Think about all the evil that's already in this world and then realize how much the Lord is currently limiting Satan's power. During the Tribulation, God will still be in control, but he will be using Satan and his forces to accomplish his own righteous judgment.

How is it that God uses evil to accomplish his purposes? Paul reminds us in Romans 9:17a that the Lord **told Pharaoh, 'I have appointed you for the very purpose of displaying my power.'** God doesn't force anyone to be evil any more than he forces anyone to repent and live righteously. He gives us all choice. But he also knows our hearts, and he knew that Pharaoh's stubborn heart would refuse to release the Israelites until God's mighty power forced him to do so.

Satan chose to rebel against God and one-third of heaven's angels went along with him. But unlike humans, there is no forgiveness, no grace, no mercy for fallen angels. Why not? (1) They lived in the very presence of God and still chose to turn against him. And (2) they, unlike humans, aren't created in God's image.

Knowing how badly we mess up and still find forgiveness through our merciful Heavenly Father, no wonder the devil and his followers hate us so much! In spite of all our sins, God loves us and continues to forgive us and promise us a heavenly home. While Satan and his demons are spending forever in torment, we'll be spending eternity where they once lived and will never live again. No wonder he's eager to see humans meet the same eternal fate as his own.

Note what is said about these four angels: They've **been prepared for this hour and day and month and year.** Only God knows when this time will be, but he is perfect and his timing is perfect, so at the appointed time, these four angels will be **turned loose to kill.**

But as terrible as all this sounds, don't overlook the continuing mercy of God. These instruments of judgment are restrained by the hand of God so they are only allowed to kill **one-third of all the people on earth.**

I heard the size of their army, which was 200 million mounted troops. Never has there been an army of such proportions. While some speculate that this is a literal human army, it's very possible that this entire force is made up of the demons John previously described as **locusts** in Revelation 9:7a: **The locusts looked like horses prepared for battle.**

Terror, terror, terror (Revelation 8:13b) beyond imagination will overwhelm those left behind. Please be ready to leave here when Jesus calls for his Church to come home.

Day 65

Yesterday we read about *the four angels who had been prepared for this hour and day and month and year* [who] *were turned loose to kill one-third of all the people on earth* (Revelation 9:15). This demonic foursome brought with them an *army, which was 200 million mounted troops* (Revelation 9:16b).

John continues: *And in my vision, I saw the horses and the riders sitting on them. The riders wore armor that was fiery red and dark blue and yellow. The horses had heads like lions, and fire and smoke and burning sulfur billowed from their mouths* (Revelation 9:17).

As I said yesterday, it's highly unlikely that this is a human army. More probably, it's the vast horde of demons John previously described as *locusts* in Revelation 9:7. John goes on to describe the *fire and smoke and burning sulfur* as *plagues* inflicted on the people remaining on Earth. (Remember, the 144,000 special witnesses are still on Earth, but have God's protection over them.)

One-third of all the people on earth were killed by these three plagues—by the fire and smoke and burning sulfur that came from the mouths of the horses. Their power was in their mouths and in their tails. For their tails had heads like snakes, with the power to injure people (Revelation 9:18-19).

The people remaining on Earth will have already been through mindboggling horror at this point. John tells us how they respond to this latest terror: *But the people who did not die in these plagues still refused to repent of their evil deeds and turn to God. They continued to worship demons and idols made of*

131

gold, silver, bronze, stone, and wood—idols that can neither see nor hear nor walk! And they did not repent of their murders or their witchcraft or their sexual immorality or their thefts (Revelation 9:20).

[G]old, silver, bronze, stone, and wood. I don't believe this is simply referring to worshiping the false gods of other religions. I think this is also talking about stuff. Material things. Those who survive the slaughter go back to business as usual.

And they did not repent of their murders or their witchcraft or their sexual immorality or their thefts (Revelation 9:21). What a God-forsaken world it will be during the Tribulation! *Thefts* will take place on an unprecedented scale because people will take whatever they want from anyone they can overpower. *Murders* will be rampant because people will kill to get what they can't simply steal. The weak, the sick, the elderly will become easy prey.

Sexual immorality will escalate to the point that no one will be safe. As terrible as sex crimes can be in this day and time, imagine living in a world with absolutely no morals and demonic forces multiplied beyond our comprehension. Look at Genesis 19 and Judges 19. If immorality in that day can be so blatant, it's absolutely nauseating to think of the immorality and perversion that will be rampant on Earth during the Tribulation.

I left *witchcraft* for last because I believe what we're seeing today is leading directly into the epidemic drug use that will be taking place during the Tribulation. What does one have to do with the other? The word *witchcraft* is translated directly from the same root word from which we get the word *pharmacy*. Drugs.

We see on the news and experience in our own families what lengths drug addicts will go to in order to get their next high. With thieves, murderers, drug addicts, and perverts all over the Earth, no one will be safe. And no one in their right mind will want to be here.

Today is the day of salvation (2 Corinthians 6:2b). *Believe in the Lord Jesus and you will be saved* (Acts 16:31a).

132

Revelation 10

Day 66

We've seen what a God-forsaken world the Tribulation time will be on Earth. Six of the designated angels have blown their trumpets. One more remains, but we won't see him until the last half of Chapter 11.

Then I saw another mighty angel coming down from heaven, surrounded by a cloud, with a rainbow over his head. His face shone like the sun, and his feet were like pillars of fire. And in his hand was a small scroll that had been opened. He stood with his right foot on the sea and his left foot on the land. And he gave a great shout like the roar of a lion. And when he shouted, the seven thunders answered. When the seven thunders spoke, I was about to write. But I heard a voice from heaven saying, 'Keep secret what the seven thunders said, and do not write it down' (Revelation 10:1-4).

In Revelation 5, we saw the Lamb of God take a scroll which only he could open. This doesn't appear to be the same scroll, since this one is described as *a small scroll*. And this isn't Jesus, since this passage identifies him as *another mighty angel*, although not one of the seven angels with trumpets.

This powerful angel *stood with his right foot on the sea and his left foot on the land.* His stance shows us that he represents God's authority over all things. *And when he shouted, the seven thunders answered.* Whoever or whatever these *thunders* are or represent, John was forbidden from writing down their words.

Why? While the Lord chose to reveal through John much of what would happen during the Last Days, he certainly didn't reveal everything. Our Creator owes us no explanations, but he is kind, loving, and merciful and offers us a wealth of information in the form of his Word, the Bible, and through the whispers of the Holy Spirit to prepare us for every moment of our lives. We don't need to know all the answers. What we do need is an unshakable trust in our Savior.

"Then the angel I saw standing on the sea and on the land raised his right hand toward heaven. He swore an oath in the name of the one who lives forever and ever, who created the heavens and everything in them, the earth and everything in it, and the sea and everything in it. He said, 'There will be no more delay. When the seventh angel blows his trumpet, God's mysterious plan will be fulfilled. It will happen just as he announced it to his servants the prophets' (Revelation 10:5-7).

[N]o more delay. This lull or break in the blowing of the trumpets may be another opportunity for the unsaved inhabitants of Earth to repent and turn to Jesus, because after *the seventh angel blows his trumpet*, time will be up.

And then *God's mysterious plan will be fulfilled. It will happen just as he announced it to his servants the prophets.* God's ways may be *mysterious*, but he has graciously provided us with a road map of his plan from beginning to end. From Genesis to Revelation, the Bible points us to Jesus. And in John 14:16b, Jesus promised us an *Advocate, who will never leave* us: his Holy Spirit.

Some translations use the word "Helper." Others say "Comforter" or "Counselor." All are speaking of the Holy Spirit, who also teaches us as we study God's Word and pray and seek his guidance. Revelation may be confusing, but we can glean enough from it to understand what lies ahead for the saved and the unsaved. And that should certainly produce in us an urgency to share what we know with others.

134

Day 67

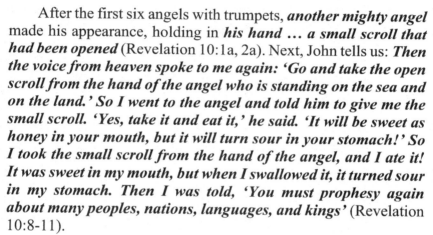

After the first six angels with trumpets, *another mighty angel* made his appearance, holding in *his hand ... a small scroll that had been opened* (Revelation 10:1a, 2a). Next, John tells us: *Then the voice from heaven spoke to me again: 'Go and take the open scroll from the hand of the angel who is standing on the sea and on the land.' So I went to the angel and told him to give me the small scroll. 'Yes, take it and eat it,' he said. 'It will be sweet as honey in your mouth, but it will turn sour in your stomach!' So I took the small scroll from the hand of the angel, and I ate it! It was sweet in my mouth, but when I swallowed it, it turned sour in my stomach. Then I was told, 'You must prophesy again about many peoples, nations, languages, and kings'* (Revelation 10:8-11).

John is told to *Go and take the open scroll ... and eat it.* This isn't as strange as it may sound (see Ezekiel 3). What was the scroll? God's message. Why was John to *eat it*? Because a person can't give out the Word unless he first takes in the Word, and John had been instructed to *prophesy again about many peoples, nations, languages, and kings.*

But what happened when John ate the scroll? *It was sweet in my mouth, but when I swallowed it, it turned sour in my stomach.*

The Word of God is sweet. Precious. But it can also be upsetting. Even terrifying. Although we're never specifically told what the little scroll contained, it was surely more information concerning the Last Days.

For John, this had to be a double-edged sword. On one hand, he was privileged with sharing God's message and pointing more people to heaven. On the other hand, he was seeing the terrible events to come and the final outcome for those who chose to reject Jesus. And that had to be upsetting.

If it was upsetting for John, it certainly ought to be upsetting for us as well. How can we say we love anyone and neglect to warn them about what happens to people who die without knowing Jesus as Lord and Savior? The Bible isn't a fairy tale. Revelation isn't fiction. It's real. And its events are headed our way. We need to be prepared and help prepare others.

Revelation 11

Day 68

Chapter 10 of the Book of Revelation closes with John being told to ***prophesy again about many peoples, nations, languages, and kings*** (Revelation 10:11). Next, John tells us: ***Then I was given a measuring stick, and I was told, 'Go and measure the Temple of God and the altar, and count the number of worshipers. But do not measure the outer courtyard, for it has been turned over to the nations. They will trample the holy city for 42 months'*** (Revelation 11:1-2).

What ***Temple of God*** is this passage referring to? Not one in existence today and not one that was in existence in John's day, but a temple that will be built in the future. This temple will be built on Mount Moriah, the same mountain on which Abraham was willing to sacrifice his son Isaac (see Genesis 22), and the same location as the previous ***Temple of God***, which stood on Mount Moriah, the Temple Mount, and was destroyed in AD 70. This is where, after Muslims conquered Jerusalem in the seventh century AD, the Islamic shrine, the Dome of the Rock, was built in AD 691 and still stands today, along with the Al-Aqsa Mosque.

There's a lot of recent history concerning this area, so bear with me while I hit the highlights. The Babylonians conquered Israel, and Israel ceased to exist as an independent nation after 606 BC (also called BCE—"before the common era," but I prefer BC—"before Christ"). Remember, in time, 606 BC came after

691 BC because time is counted down rather than up until we get to AD (also called CE—the "common era", but I prefer AD—"Anno Domini," meaning "in the year of our Lord"). It wasn't until AD 1948—a very short time ago when looking at the big picture—that Israel was again recognized as an independent nation.

Back to our passage. John is told, *count the number of worshipers*. What are these worshipers doing? When that temple is built, it will be a remake of the previous or original temple, including the altars and priests trained in the proper procedures for fulfilling the daily sacrifices. To continue to offer sacrifices for the sins of the people is to deny the once-and-for-all sacrifice made by Jesus Christ, so anyone worshiping at this temple will not believe that Jesus Christ was and is God. They may be worshiping, but just like the folks who'll be next door at the Al-Aqsa Mosque, they'll be turning their backs on the only one who can save them.

But do not measure the outer courtyard. While it was long believed that the Dome of the Rock was built directly on the site of the last temple, more recent archaeological studies indicate that the Dome of the Rock is actually located in what would be the *outer courtyard* of the temple, the area that was known as the Court of the Gentiles.

[F]or it has been turned over to the nations. They will trample the holy city for 42 months. I know these flip-flops in time are very confusing, but hold on and I'll do my best to unravel this as we go along. I believe the Rapture of the Church will occur soon after the temple is rebuilt, and the Jews who are left behind during the Tribulation will be an especially persecuted group. Jerusalem will be a high priority target and will be trampled for *42 months*, the last half of the Tribulation period.

Tomorrow we'll meet the *two witnesses* (Revelation 11:3) who will have a special purpose during this time.

Day 69

Yesterday we read about the temple John was shown, a temple that didn't exist in his time and doesn't exist today, but rather a temple that will be built in the future on the Temple Mount in Jerusalem. During the Tribulation, Jerusalem will be a high priority target and will be trampled *for 42 months* (Revelation 11:2b), the last half of the Tribulation period.

John continues: *I was told ... 'And I will give power to my two witnesses, and they will be clothed in burlap and will prophesy during those 1,260 days'* (Revelation 11:1a, 3). This is the first mention of these *two witnesses* in the Book of Revelation, but we are told quite a bit about them in the very first sentence:

(1) They will be given *power*. These two men—the original language clearly indicates they are both male and human—are specially empowered for their ministry.

(2) *[T]hey will be clothed in burlap.* In Biblical times, people wore burlap as a sign of repentance. Their own salvation is evidenced in the wearing of *burlap*—called "sackcloth" in some translations.

And (3) they *will prophecy during those 1,260 days*, the last three and a half years or *42 months* of the Tribulation.

These two prophets are the two olive trees and the two lampstands that stand before the Lord of all the earth (Revelation 11:4).

If we look in the Old Testament, we see a vision given to the prophet Zechariah concerning this future time. An angel appeared to Zechariah: *'What do you see?'* he asked. *'I see a solid gold lampstand,'* I replied, *'with a bowl at the top and seven lamps on it, with seven spouts to each of the lamps. There are also two olive trees beside it, one on the right of the bowl and the other on its left.' Then I asked the angel, 'What are the two olive trees on the right and left of the lampstand?' ... he said, 'These are the two anointed ones who are standing beside the Lord of all the earth'* (from Zechariah 4).

How is it that these two witnesses are human yet stand *beside the Lord of all the earth*? Many believe them to be Moses and Elijah sent for this special mission. Others speculate they could be Elijah and Enoch, since both were taken into heaven without experiencing physical death (see Genesis 5:24 and 2 Kings 2:11). Whomever they are, they're no ordinary humans.

But why two witnesses? In John 8:17, Jesus told the Pharisees, *Your own law says that if two people agree about something, their witness is accepted as fact.* And Hebrews 10:28 tells us that *anyone who refused to obey the law of Moses was put to death without mercy on the testimony of two or three witnesses.*

So a minimum of two witnesses was required to issue a death penalty. These two special witnesses will primarily witness against the Beast and False Prophet, and you can be sure that both of those God-haters—the Beast and False Prophet—will receive the eternal death penalty (see Revelation 19:20).

Sadly, the Beast and False Prophet won't be the only ones sentenced to eternal damnation. Tomorrow we'll see who else is included.

Day 70

We're in Chapter 11 of Revelation and we're looking at the two special witnesses God will send for the last half of the Tribulation. *[T]hey will be clothed in burlap and will prophesy during those 1,260 days* (Revelation 11:3b). These two special witnesses will primarily speak against the Beast and False Prophet.

If anyone tries to harm them, fire flashes from their mouths and consumes their enemies. This is how anyone who tries to harm them must die. They have power to shut the sky so that no rain will fall for as long as they prophesy. And they have the power to turn the rivers and oceans into blood, and to strike the earth with every kind of plague as often as they wish (Revelation 11:1a, 3-6).

During the time God has determined for these men to be on Earth warning people against putting their faith in the Beast and False Prophet, the Lord will protect these two men from all harm and allow them to perform mighty demonstrations of his power, from stopping any rain from falling to releasing deadly plagues.

When they complete their testimony, the beast that comes up out of the bottomless pit will declare war against them, and he will conquer them and kill them. And their bodies will lie in the main street of Jerusalem, the city that is figuratively called 'Sodom' and 'Egypt,' the city where their Lord was crucified. And for three and a half days, all peoples, tribes, languages, and nations will stare at their bodies. No one will be allowed to bury them. All the people who belong to this world will gloat over them and give presents to each other to celebrate the death of the two prophets who had tormented them (Revelation 11:7-10).

At God's appointed time, the two witnesses will be killed by *the beast that comes up out of the bottomless pit*, which will look like a victory for evil. The people of Earth will be so enthralled with the Beast and False Prophet (we'll learn more about them later) that they actually celebrate the deaths of the two witnesses who spoke out against them. The place of their death is clearly Jerusalem.

And for three and a half days, all peoples, tribes, languages, and nations will stare at their bodies. No one will be allowed to bury them. Never before in history has it been possible for *all peoples, tribes, languages, and nations* around the world to be able to simultaneously watch what is happening in real time in an entirely different part of the world. Today there are many ways of instant communication. Larry and I video chat regularly with our friends in Norway. We see them, they see us, and we chat away in real time. In John's day, this was unthinkable, but today it's commonplace.

God isn't finished with his two special witnesses. More on them tomorrow. Meanwhile, I'd left off yesterday by saying that the Beast and False Prophet won't be the only ones sentenced to eternal damnation.

In Matthew 25, Jesus teaches about the Final Judgment, making it crystal clear how real Christians are to conduct themselves. While many claim to belong to Jesus, the proof is in the living. And those whose conduct is contrary to his teaching, he says: *Away with you, you cursed ones, into the eternal fire prepared for the devil and his demons* (Matthew 25:41b).

Are you reading your Bible? Praying? Serving others? Supporting a local church with your presence and finances? This is what true believers in Jesus Christ are to be doing. Your kids, grandkids, coworkers, friends, and neighbors are all learning from your example. Is yours a good one to follow? Only those who truly know him will be exempt from the Tribulation.

Day 71

God's two special witnesses have completed their time of prophesying and have been killed by *the beast that comes up out of the bottomless pit* (Revelation 11:7b). Let me stop right here and say that whatever God has called you to do, do it. He will give you the strength, ability, and time to do it. Yes, the Bible says we can lengthen or shorten our days by the way we live—which is another lesson in itself—but if you're living for the Lord and doing His will, your life will continue until God says your time is up.

The time for these two special witnesses is up, and the whole world watches as the two men's bodies are left *in the main street of Jerusalem* (Revelation 11:8a). There's a global celebration since these men had been speaking out against the Beast and the False Prophet.

But after three and a half days, God breathed life into them, and they stood up! (Revelation 11:11a). Bet that'll put a halt to the celebrating. All around the world, the partyers will be glued to their computers, laptops, TVs, and phone screens watching with mouths agape. When John saw this future event, he said, *Terror struck all who were staring at them.* Don't you know it did!

And the world is in for another shock: *Then a loud voice from heaven called to the two prophets, 'Come up here!' And they rose to heaven in a cloud as their enemies watched* (Revelation 11:12). Does everyone watching hear the voice? I don't know, but they do see the two witnesses as they are visibly taken into *heaven in a cloud*.

At the same time there was a terrible earthquake that destroyed a tenth of the city. Seven thousand people died in that earthquake, and everyone else was terrified and gave glory to the God of heaven (Revelation 11:13). Isn't it pathetic how quickly we humans can change directions? One minute they're elated over the death of the two witnesses and the next minute, when an earthquake scares them silly, they're giving *glory to the God of heaven*.

That, my friends, is what's called foxhole conversion, and for many, it lasts about as long as it's taken to write this sentence. I've seen so many people on fire for Jesus one minute and living like the devil the next. But real conversion lasts. When a person sincerely accepts the Holy Spirit's invitation of salvation, his constant presence gives them the stick-with-it-ness to stay the course toward heaven.

How did Jesus put it? *Anyone who puts a hand to the plow and then looks back is not fit for the Kingdom* (Luke 9:62). Meaning what? If you mess up, you're toast? No! Jesus knows we'll mess up. He knows not one of us will get it all right. But no one who truly receives Jesus as Lord and Savior ever misses their old life and old ways. I know I make mistakes every day, but I also know I never want to go back to who I was pre-Jesus.

Real Christians are ready to go when Christ calls his Church home to glory. No one who truly knows Jesus will be left behind.

Day 72

The two special witnesses are killed, left in the street in Jerusalem, and then raised from the dead. As they're being visibly taken up into heaven, *there was a terrible earthquake that destroyed a tenth of the city. Seven thousand people died in that earthquake, and everyone else was terrified and gave glory to the God of heaven* (Revelation 11:13).

The ones who'd been celebrating the deaths of the two witnesses because they'd been speaking out against the Beast and the False Prophet suddenly decided they'd better switch sides. A lot of people do this. Let a crisis come along and suddenly they want Jesus as their best friend. Let the crisis pass, and it's back to their same old ways.

If you think back, we've seen seven special angels who had been given trumpets to blow at specific times. Six have done so and the fifth and sixth trumpets brought horrific destruction. Then, before the seventh angel blows his trumpet, the small scroll has been opened, and the two witnesses have appeared, been killed, brought back to life, and visibly taken up into heaven. All this is followed by a terrible earthquake.

Afterwards, John says: *The second terror is past, but look, the third terror is coming quickly. Then the seventh angel blew his trumpet, and there were loud voices shouting in heaven: 'The world has now become the Kingdom of our Lord and of his Christ, and he will reign forever and ever* (Revelation 11:14-15).

[T]he Kingdom of our Lord and of his Christ, and he will reign forever and ever. If you're familiar with Handel's "Messiah," you recognize this phrase from the music.

Next, John shows us a scene in heaven. Just like the people of Earth celebrated the death of the two witnesses, everyone in heaven is celebrating what's about to happen on Earth. No one is rejoicing over the destruction or horror people on Earth are enduring, but they are celebrating as God prepares to end Satan's time as *the prince of this world* (John 12:31).

The twenty-four elders sitting on their thrones before God fell with their faces to the ground and worshiped him. And they said, 'We give thanks to you, Lord God, the Almighty, the one who is and who always was, for now you have assumed your great power and have begun to reign. The nations were filled with wrath, but now the time of your wrath has come. It is time to judge the dead and reward your servants the prophets, as well as your holy people, and all who fear your name, from the least to the greatest. It is time to destroy all who have caused destruction on the earth (Revelation 11:16-18).

[T]he time of your wrath has come. The Lord's patience has ended. Those remaining on Earth have seen only the tip of the iceberg compared to what awaits them in eternity.

It is time to judge the dead and reward your servants the prophets, as well as your holy people, and all who fear your name, from the least to the greatest. God's people will be rewarded, but those who have rejected him will soon stand at the Great White Throne of Judgment and hear their eternal damnation pronounced.

It is time to destroy all who have caused destruction on the earth. What kind of destruction is this verse talking about? More than anything else, I believe it's talking about those whose lives have led people away from faith in Christ. Every person influences someone, and that influence either points people to Jesus or draws them farther from him.

When the time of God's wrath comes, where will you be? If you know Jesus, you'll be one of those celebrating in heaven.

Day 73

The seventh angel has blown his trumpet and all heaven has begun celebrating the end of Satan's time as *the prince of this world* (John 12:31). *Then, in heaven, the Temple of God was opened and the Ark of his covenant could be seen inside the Temple. Lightning flashed, thunder crashed and roared, and there was an earthquake and a terrible hailstorm* (Revelation 11:19).

In the earthly Temple, the Ark of the Covenant—the chest containing the Ten Commandments, a jar of manna, and Aaron's rod that budded (see Hebrews 9:4)—represented the presence and the faithfulness of God. The cover of the Ark of the Covenant was the mercy seat, or bema, representing the throne of God. God himself covers us with his love and protection and fulfills every promise he makes. This was the place of atonement, and God himself in the form of Jesus Christ atoned for our sins through his own death. In heaven, John now sees the actual Temple and Ark, not the earthly representations that had once stood in Jerusalem.

Lightning flashed, thunder crashed and roared, and there was an earthquake and a terrible hailstorm. In Exodus 19 we read: *Then the Lord told Moses, 'Go down and prepare the people for my arrival. So Moses went down to the people. He consecrated them for worship .... On the morning of the third day, thunder roared and lightning flashed, and a dense cloud came down on the mountain* (verses 10a, 14a, 16a). In the Exodus passage, the Lord was meeting with his own people. In Revelation, the Lord is coming to deal with those who don't belong to him.

Note, too, that at the foot of Mount Sinai—the place where the Exodus 19 passage takes place—the Lord is hidden within *a dense cloud*. When Jesus returns to Earth, he will be with the clouds, but not hidden by them: ***Behold, he cometh with clouds; and every eye shall see him*** (Revelation 1:7a, KJV).

Don't confuse his Second Coming with the Rapture. In the Rapture, the Church is taken up into glory; Jesus doesn't set foot on the Earth. He calls his own to join him in heaven. In the Second Coming, Jesus returns to Earth, along with all his people, to end the reign of *the prince of this world* after the seven years of the Tribulation.

If Jesus calls his people home today, will you be ready? Who do you know that won't be? Don't put off talking to them about Jesus.

Revelation 12

Day 74

Chapter 12 opens: ***Then I witnessed in heaven an event of great significance. I saw a woman clothed with the sun, with the moon beneath her feet, and a crown of twelve stars on her head. She was pregnant, and she cried out because of her labor pains and the agony of giving birth*** (Revelation 12:1-2).

This ***woman*** is the first of the seven featured players we'll be introduced to in Chapters 12 through 14: (1) the woman, Israel; (2) the dragon, Satan; (3) the male child the woman gives birth to, Jesus; (4) Michael, the angel in charge of heaven's angels; (5) the rest of the woman's children, the Gentiles who turn to Jesus during the Tribulation; (6) the beast out of the sea, the Antichrist; and (7) the beast out of the earth, the false prophet.

In John's vision, there were twelve stars on the woman's head, representing the twelve tribes of Israel. While some see this woman as the Virgin Mary, the rest of the passage and related events make it very clear that the woman represents not the individual mother of Jesus, but the nation of Israel who ***cried out because of her labor pains and the agony of giving birth*** as the son of God was brought into the world through the nation of Israel. At that time, Israel was suffering greatly under the rule of the Romans.

Israel has always had and continues to have a significant role in God's plan. As Psalm 122:6 reminds us, we're to ***[p]ray for*** *peace in Jerusalem.* And this same passage goes on to say: *May all who love this city prosper.* God will never bless the nation or person who turns his back on Israel.

The turmoil in Israel today is indicative of the time we're living in. The Rapture is on the horizon. Be ready.

Day 75

Yesterday we started Chapter 12. Today we continue: ***Then I witnessed in heaven another significant event. I saw a large red dragon with seven heads and ten horns, with seven crowns on his heads*** (Revelation 12:3).

The dragon, representing Satan, is seen with **seven heads and ten horns, with seven crowns on his heads**. Everything in this description depicts arrogance, bloodthirstiness, and a desire for power. Satan wants to be seen as all-powerful—seven being the number of perfection or completeness—and having all authority. Thus the seven crowns. He wants to be recognized as the ultimate ruler rather than the loser he is.

As a side note, there's another lesson in this description. Anytime someone has to blow their own horn, flash their own bling, and demand attention, beware. While Satan wants to be flashy and noticed, wants power and authority, the humble Savior came in human form with no fanfare, no demands for power or authority, nothing whatsoever except redeeming love and grace and mercy. His is the example we should follow.

His tail swept away one-third of the stars in the sky, and he threw them to the earth (Revelation 12:4a). When the angel Lucifer turned against his Creator, he was cast from heaven to earth, along with those who followed him in his rebellion, one-third of the heavenly angels. Angels, unlike humans, aren't made in the image of God and aren't granted the astounding privilege available to humans: grace and forgiveness. No wonder Satan and the corrupted angels who became his demons hate humans so much: sinful, bumbling man can be forgiven with the whisper of one heartfelt prayer.

He stood in front of the woman as she was about to give birth, ready to devour her baby as soon as it was born (Revelation 12:4b). Satan used Herod to seek Jesus' death as soon as he was born. Matthew 2:1 tells us that *wise men from eastern lands* came to Herod and asked where they could find the newborn King. Herod consulted the priests and religious teachers and learned that prophecy said the child would be born in Bethlehem, so he told the wise men to let him know when they found the child *so that I can go and worship him, too!* (Matthew 2:8b).

When the wise men failed to report back to him, lying ol' Herod *sent soldiers to kill all the boys in and around Bethlehem who were two years old and under, based on the wise men's report of the star's first appearance* (Matthew 2:16b).

Contrary to the nativity scenes we see, the wise men didn't show up at the stable alongside the shepherds. By the time they arrived, Mary and Joseph were living in a house, and Jesus was a toddler (see Matthew 2:11). This explains why Herod ordered the murder of the male babies all the way up to age two.

Herod's plan, which had been Satan's plan, failed, of course. But it's significant to note that Satan found a willing participant in the power-hungry Herod. Satan can and will use anyone—even a believer in Jesus—who isn't fully covered in the armor of God (see Ephesians 6:13-17).

Are you suited up in God's armor? I sure hope so. You're on the battlefield, believer. And you need to be in daily communication with your Commander.

Day 76

Yesterday we looked at the dragon, representing Satan, who *stood in front of the woman as she was about to give birth, ready to devour her baby as soon as it was born* (Revelation 12:4b). The woman, we saw, represented Israel bringing forth the Messiah. Satan, using Herod, as well as direct temptations, wanted, more than anything, to destroy Jesus.

Israel *gave birth to a son who was to rule all nations with an iron rod* (Revelation 12:5a). The tiny baby Jesus came to save the world—all those who would put their faith in him—but he also came to judge the world.

And her child was snatched away from the dragon and was caught up to God and to his throne (Revelation 12:5b). Jesus Christ wasn't murdered on the cross. He went there willingly and he died willingly as the One Perfect Sacrifice for our sins. He was then returned to his rightful place, *caught up to God and to his throne*.

And the woman fled into the wilderness, where God had prepared a place to care for her for 1,260 days (Revelation 12:6). We're in a difficult part of the Revelation. While Verse 5 deals with past events, Verse 6 looks to the future when the believers in Israel will become a special target of the evil forces at work during the Tribulation. Because of this and because nothing takes God by surprise, he has already *prepared a place to care for her for 1,260 days*, the final three and a half years of the Tribulation.

I'll stop here for now because we're wading into even deeper waters tomorrow. Note the last passage included above: The Lord *prepared a place*. Sound familiar? In John 14:2b, Jesus told his disciples, ***I am going away to prepare a place for you*** (HCSB). He's doing that for every person who has put their trust in him. Have you? If you have, your home in heaven is waiting.

Day 77

Then there was war in heaven. Michael and his angels fought against the dragon and his angels. And the dragon lost the battle, and he and his angels were forced out of heaven. This great dragon—the ancient serpent called the devil, or Satan, the one deceiving the whole world—was thrown down to the earth with all his angels (Revelation 12:7-9).

As hard as it is to swallow, Satan still has access to heaven. How else can he be called our *accuser*? See Revelation 12:10. At the time of his rebellion against God, he was cast out of his position as a heavenly angel—heaven was no longer his home—but he retained access to heaven only as our *accuser*. Case in point, look at Job: *[T]he members of the heavenly court came to present themselves before the Lord, and the Accuser, Satan, came with them* (Job 1:6).

Halfway through the Tribulation, that access will be stripped from him. John watched as *Michael and his angels fought against the dragon and his angels*. The Lord doesn't have to speak a word or lift a finger to defeat Satan. Michael, the heavenly counterpart to the evil Lucifer, or Satan, is more than capable of dealing with the devil. As this passage tells us: *[T]he dragon lost the battle, and he and his angels were forced out of heaven.*

As we saw a few days ago, when the angel Lucifer rebelled against God, he took with him one-third of the heavenly angels (see Revelation 12:4). That leaves two-thirds still faithful to the Lord and under the command of Michael. Satan may have an army, but God has a bigger one.

Satan so enjoys accusing God's people of wrongdoing. When he loses his access to heaven, he loses that final pleasure and is left with nothing but boiling hatred for the humans who are made in God's image.

So if you think things are bad now, wait until the midpoint of the Tribulation and see how awful the world becomes. Of course, if you've committed your life to Jesus, you won't be here because, before the Tribulation begins, the Rapture will take place and you'll be taken home to Jesus. But for those who don't belong to Christ, the Tribulation horrors await.

Let me leave you with this thought: You're watching your favorite TV program when a news bulletin breaks in, stating that a heavily armed gang of escaped murderers is shooting their way through your neighborhood and headed your way. Will you take shelter? Or let's say they're headed toward your friend's house. Or your son's. Or daughter's. Or grandchild's. Will you warn them?

There is no safe shelter outside the arms of Jesus, and there is no one who doesn't deserve to be warned about the coming time of horror on this earth. Do your part. Live for Jesus. Pray for others. And urge them to turn to Jesus while there's still time.

Day 78

Finally, Satan's access to heaven has been fully closed, and this is what happens next: ***Then I heard a loud voice shouting across the heavens, 'It has come at last—salvation and power and the Kingdom of our God, and the authority of his Christ. For the accuser of our brothers and sisters has been thrown down to earth—the one who accuses them before our God day and night. And they have defeated him by the blood of the Lamb and by their testimony. And they did not love their lives so much that they were afraid to die.***

Therefore, rejoice, O heavens! And you who live in the heavens, rejoice! But terror will come on the earth and the sea, for the devil has come down to you in great anger, knowing that he has little time' (Revelation 12:10-12).

Who is this ***loud voice shouting across the heavens***? All the saints of heaven, every person who has put their faith in Christ. How can we know this? Look at what they say: ***[T]he accuser of our brothers and sisters has been thrown down to earth—the one who accuses them before our God day and night.***

Satan knows and has always known that he's on a short leash. His time is limited. His power is limited. His eternal punishment is drawing closer and closer, and he's desperately clawing at every opportunity to turn others away from faith in Jesus.

Which is why we need a good defense attorney. And, believe me, we have the very best. First John 2:1b reminds us: ***[W]e have an advocate who pleads our case before the Father. He is Jesus Christ, the one who is truly righteous.*** There's no better representation than that.

So how do these saints of God say they've received the victory?

(1) *[B]y the blood of the Lamb.* As Jesus said in John 14:6b: *No one comes to the Father except through me* (BSB). Only because of Christ's sacrificial death on the cross was salvation made possible. Only through faith in him as the One and Only Son of God can anyone spend eternity in heaven. Do you have that faith?

(2) *[B]y their testimony.* It's obvious when you're in love with Jesus. You live by his teachings and you tell others how he can give them new life that lasts forever. How does your daily testimony honor the Savior?

(3) *And they did not love their lives so much that they were afraid to die.* The shout heard in this passage may be voiced as one, but I have a feeling the Tribulation saints and those from the Middle East and countries like North Korea and Somalia will be at the forefront.

It's easy to say what we think we'd do in a situation where our faith is challenged, but let's be honest here: we don't really know what we'd do until we're faced with that decision. One thing I do know for sure, though: if Jesus isn't important enough to talk about in your daily life, he sure isn't important enough to risk dying for. How important is Jesus to you?

Day 79

When the dragon realized that he had been thrown down to the earth, he pursued the woman who had given birth to the male child. But she was given two wings like those of a great eagle so she could fly to the place prepared for her in the wilderness. There she would be cared for and protected from the dragon for a time, times, and half a time (Revelation 12:13-14).

Once again, we see the woman, representing Israel, being the target of Satan's wrath. Why? The Messiah came through the Jews. The Jews are God's chosen people. Nothing has changed that. And since this passage refers to the midpoint of the Tribulation, we can safely say that this woman particularly represents the Jews who have put their faith in the Lord Jesus after the time of the Rapture.

But she was given two wings like those of a great eagle so she could fly to the place prepared for her in the wilderness. Whether this is an airplane or a supernaturally empowered eagle or something entirely different, God has already *prepared a place to care for her* (Revelation 12:6). And when God makes a plan, it's unthwartable (and I just invented that word because it's the strongest adjective I could think of). Satan's forces can't defeat the protection God has already prepared for this remnant of Israel: *[T]here is a remnant chosen by grace* (Romans 11:5b, NIV).

There she would be cared for and protected from the dragon for a time, times, and half a time (Revelation 12:14). As we've already seen in a previous passage, this refers to the last three and half years of the Tribulation: *And the woman fled into the wilderness, where God had prepared a place to care for her for 1,260 days* (Revelation 12:6).

Then the dragon tried to drown the woman with a flood of water that flowed from his mouth (Revelation 12:15). What happened when Peter tried to walk on water? *[H]e began to sink* (Matthew 14:30). And what did Jesus do? *Jesus immediately reached out and grabbed him* (Matthew 14:31). When we are in right standing with God, his protection is in place. Israel may be a target of Satan, but these Tribulation believers are under the protection of their Savior.

But the earth helped her by opening its mouth and swallowing the river that gushed out from the mouth of the dragon (Revelation 12:16). In Psalm 69:15a, David cried out: *Don't let the floods overwhelm me, or the deep waters swallow me.* And in Psalm 32:7, he says: *For you are my hiding place; you protect me from trouble. You surround me with songs of victory.* No matter how deep your troubles seem, when you're committed to Jesus, you're not alone. And for these Tribulation believers, God, who's in control of everything, eliminates Satan's flood simply by commanding the earth to open up and swallow it.

Don Moen opens a great song of praise with this familiar line: "God will make a way where there seems to be no way" ("God Will Make a Way," 1990). And that's exactly what He does. For me. For you. For all His people.

Day 80

And the dragon was angry at the woman and declared war against the rest of her children—all who keep God's commandments and maintain their testimony for Jesus (Revelation 12:17).

Here she is again, the woman who represents Israel. Many people will wait until after the Rapture to put their faith in Jesus Christ, but the Jewish believers who do so will be under a special protection. Today's passage, though, says that *the dragon*, representing Satan, *declared war against the rest of* the woman's *children.*

Who are these *children*? Non-Jewish believers who have come to Christ during the Tribulation and have not yet been slaughtered. Paul says in Galatians 6:14b-16: *God forbid that I should glory in anything except the Cross of our Lord Jesus Christ.... For neither circumcision nor uncircumcision is of any importance; but only a renewed nature. And all who shall regulate their lives by this principle—may peace and mercy be given to them—and to the true Israel of God* (Weymouth New Testament).

Look again at today's Revelation passage and see John's identification of *the rest of her children—all who keep God's commandments and maintain their testimony for Jesus.* We can't judge other people's hearts, but as Jesus taught in Matthew 7:20: *[Y]ou can identify a tree by its fruit, so you can identify people by their actions.*

161

What you say you believe is confirmed by your actions. Do you love Jesus? If you do, then you serve him. You may not teach or preach, but neither do you sit on your proverbial laurels and do nothing. Even if you're homebound, you can make phone calls, send texts, online messages, and cards of encouragement. If you're breathing and alive in Jesus, you have work to do.

Right after Jesus spoke about identifying *people by their actions*, he issued a stern warning: *Not everyone who calls out to me, 'Lord! Lord!' will enter the Kingdom of Heaven. Only those who actually do the will of my Father in heaven will enter* (Matthew 7:21).

This is the key. This is the evidence. This is the proof of a person's true salvation. A person who has sincerely committed their heart and life to Jesus does God's will.

And that's no mystery. Look at more of Jesus' teachings: *[I]f you do good only to those who do good to you, why should you get credit? Even sinners do that much! Love your enemies! Do good to them. You must be compassionate, just as your Father is compassionate* (Luke 6:33, 35a, 36).

Did you get that? *You must be compassionate, just as your Father is compassionate.* Compassion isn't an option. Compassion is clear evidence of discipleship. I have spoken to quite a few professing Christians who basically say that "compassion isn't my thing." According to the Word of God, it is if you belong to Jesus.

The one verse we started with today deserves a little more coverage before I move on, but I'll save the rest for tomorrow. For now, this is a good time to ask the Lord to examine your heart and show you your true level of compassion.

Day 81

Today we wrap up our look at this verse: *And the dragon was angry at the woman and declared war against the rest of her children—all who keep God's commandments and maintain their testimony for Jesus* (Revelation 12:17).

Those who wait until the Tribulation to commit their lives to Jesus will be persecuted, tortured, and killed, but they will *maintain their testimony for Jesus*. As Revelation 12:11 tells us: *[T]hey did not love their lives so much that they were afraid to die.*

How about you and me? Do we love our lives more than we love Jesus Christ? Are we *afraid to die* for our faith? Me, I'm petrified at the thought! But here's the thing: when you trust the Lord, he gives you what you need when you need it. Not before, but when.

Let me give you the condensed version of a personal experience. I was teaching a group of pastors in China—an illegal meeting—when police and military vehicles came swarming into the apartment complex where we were. Guns drawn. Running everywhere. Pounding on doors. Someone had reported seeing two white women and they had come to see what we were up to.

It had been an all-day project just to get people into the apartment inconspicuously. People had come one at a time for hours, some in their 70s riding bicycles for as long as eight hours just to be there. Now the apartment was packed wall to wall and our lookout cried out in terror when she saw what was happening outside our door.

As a born coward, I can take credit for absolutely nothing. But at that point, ***the peace of God, which surpasses all understanding*** (Philippians 4:7a, ESV), absolutely overwhelmed me, and I began to speak through my translator, calming everyone as I told them about Elisha when the king of Aram surrounded the city and Elisha's servant was struck with terror.

When the servant of the man of God got up early the next morning and went outside, there were troops, horses, and chariots everywhere. 'Oh, sir, what will we do now?' the young man cried to Elisha. 'Don't be afraid!' Elisha told him. 'For there are more on our side than on theirs.' Then Elisha prayed, 'O Lord, open his eyes and let him see!' The Lord opened the young man's eyes, and when he looked up, he saw that the hillside around Elisha was filled with horses and chariots of fire (2 Kings 6:15-17).

As everyone listened, one after one, the pastors began to sing "Amazing Grace" in Chinese. Never have I heard a more beautiful sound. And whether the Lord blinded those men from seeing our door or caused the door to be invisible, or covered it with angels, I don't know. But that one single door was never knocked on.

I and the people with me experienced God's protection and peace in a miraculous way. And here's what I don't want you to miss: we experienced that peace before we had any idea whether or not those soldiers would come in and kill us or take us all to prison. It wasn't peace that we would be kept from danger. It was peace in spite of the danger.

That same peace is available to every believer. You've heard this before, but it bears repeating: He may not calm the storm, but he will calm the child. Only trust him.

Day 82

Then the dragon took his stand on the shore beside the sea. Then I saw a beast rising up out of the sea. It had seven heads and ten horns, with ten crowns on its horns. And written on each head were names that blasphemed God (Revelation 12:18, 13:1).

Note that the ***dragon*** and the ***beast*** are two different creatures even though they both are said to have ***seven heads and ten horns***. If we look back at Revelation 12, we can compare the description of the dragon, representing Satan, with that of the beast seen in today's passage:

Then I witnessed in heaven another significant event. I saw a large red dragon with seven heads and ten horns, with seven crowns on his heads (Revelation 12:3). Seven heads, seven crowns. Seven, the number of completion or perfection. Satan desires to be all-powerful.

While the dragon John saw had ***seven crowns on his heads***, the beast has ***ten crowns on its horns***. Horns signify power, so these are clearly two very powerful beings. The ***ten crowns*** seen on the beast seem to indicate ten seats of power or nations over which the beast will rule.

First and foremost, though, the ***dragon*** imagery speaks of cunning and intelligence. A ***beast***, on the other hand, indicates less brain and more brawn. In other words, the beast will take his orders from the dragon.

And written on each head were names that blasphemed God. This beast openly speaks against God. More than that, he flaunts his hatred of Jesus Christ and pours out his rage on anyone who dares to claim Jesus Christ as Lord and Savior.

This beast looked like a leopard, but it had the feet of a bear and the mouth of a lion! And the dragon gave the beast his own power and throne and great authority (Revelation 13:2).

This description is similar to what Daniel saw (see Daniel 7) in his end-time vision, with each animal representing a different characteristic: (1) leopard—an animal who sneaks up on its prey; (2) bear—slow, but powerful, able to crush its prey; (3) lion—ferocious and roaring, announcing its presence and power.

Who is this beast that Satan, the dragon, would actually confer *his own power and throne and great authority* over to him? We'll learn more about him tomorrow. Please pray for wisdom and understanding as we continue this study.

Revelation 13

Day 83

Let's review and add more to our passage from yesterday: *Then I saw a beast rising up out of the sea. It had seven heads and ten horns, with ten crowns on its horns. And written on each head were names that blasphemed God. This beast looked like a leopard, but it had the feet of a bear and the mouth of a lion! And the dragon gave the beast his own power and throne and great authority.*

I saw that one of the heads of the beast seemed wounded beyond recovery—but the fatal wound was healed! The whole world marveled at this miracle and gave allegiance to the beast. They worshiped the dragon for giving the beast such power, and they also worshiped the beast. 'Who is as great as the beast?' they exclaimed. 'Who is able to fight against him?' (Revelation 13:1-4).

We know the dragon represents Satan, and we know that Satan has given over *his own power and throne and great authority* to the *beast rising up out of the sea*. Thus, we're looking at a picture of the Antichrist. Somehow this man—and he is indeed a man—is mortally wounded and yet survives. As John tells us, the beast's *fatal wound was healed!*

We need to understand that this beast, or Antichrist, is an imitator of Christ. Just as Jesus died and rose again, so does the Antichrist, and *[t]he whole world marveled at this miracle and gave allegiance to the beast.* That same passage goes on to tell us they *worshiped the dragon* and *worshiped the beast*.

All that said, how do we know the Antichrist is a man? For one thing, the Apostle Paul identifies him as *the son of lawlessness* (2 Thessalonians 2:3). And coming up later in this same chapter, John will tell us: *Let the one with understanding solve the meaning of the number of the beast, for it is the number of a man* (Revelation 13:18b).

What about the worship of the dragon? As we saw when the demonic horde was released after the fifth angel blew his trumpet, the dragon is clearly identified as Satan himself: *Their king is the angel from the bottomless pit; his name in Hebrew is Abaddon, and in Greek, Apollyon—the Destroyer* (Revelation 9:11).

Allow me to pause right here and remind us all that the Antichrist will appear as a charmer. He won't be hideous. He'll seem like a savior. And for a person who doesn't know Jesus and doesn't know the Bible, he's going to seem to be the one who can put the world back in order. All the Earth will be in turmoil, and this man is going to promise to make things better, when his entire plan is actually nothing but destruction.

I must keep saying this: if you aren't 100 percent sure of your salvation through faith in Jesus Christ, you need to get that settled right here and now. True salvation isn't merely a one-time experience where you confess Jesus as Lord and that covers all the bases. True salvation means that confession is the starting point of a lifelong desire to grow in and live that newfound faith. As Jesus put it: *[T]he one who endures to the end will be saved* (Mark 13:13b).

While no Christian is perfect, a true Christian is going to strive for consistency in their walk, talk, thought life, and prayer life. How much of your day is focused on pleasing Jesus?

Day 84

Then the beast was allowed to speak great blasphemies against God. And he was given authority to do whatever he wanted for forty-two months (Revelation 13:5).

Here's another reminder about the jumps in time in the Book of Revelation. The Antichrist will appear at the beginning of the seven years of Tribulation, but he's going to be seen as the one person who can stop all the chaos and bring order. For this reason, the world will put their trust in Him, with two exceptions: (1) The non-Jews who put their faith in Jesus after the Rapture and are going to be martyred; and (2) the Jews who put their faith in Jesus after the Rapture who will be under God's special protection.

So, after the seemingly miraculous healing of the Beast—also known as the Antichrist—the whole world *worshiped the dragon for giving the beast such power, and they also worshiped the beast* (Revelation 13:4a). And his power is an all-out dictatorship: *And he was given authority to do whatever he wanted.*

And he spoke terrible words of blasphemy against God, slandering his name and his dwelling—that is, those who dwell in heaven. And the beast was allowed to wage war against God's holy people and to conquer them. And he was given authority to rule over every tribe and people and language and nation (Revelation 13:6-7).

The Beast blasphemes not only *God ... and His dwelling* but also *those who dwell in heaven*. Those who went to be with the Lord before the Tribulation are untouchable, including those who were taken in the Rapture. And the thoughts of all those he can't get his hands on is infuriating.

So for this time, the Antichrist is ***allowed to wage war against God's holy people and to conquer them***. Who are ***God's holy people***? Those who were left behind at the time of the Rapture and have now committed their hearts and lives to Jesus. Physically, the Antichrist will conquer them; spiritually, they'll be secure in Jesus, who said it as plainly as possible: ***Don't be afraid of those who want to kill your body; they cannot touch your soul. Fear only God*** (Matthew 10:28a).

No one wants to suffer physically, but even for those who are tortured and killed for their faith in Jesus Christ, their eternal home awaits. No one or nothing has the power to ***touch your soul***. If you belong to Jesus, you're safe for eternity regardless of what you go through beforehand in this life.

As Revelation 21:4a promises every person who has put their faith in Jesus: ***He will wipe every tear from their eyes, and there will be no more death or sorrow or crying or pain.*** In heaven, anything suffered on this earth won't even be a distant memory.

I pray no one reading this will be here after the Rapture. But for those who are still here, physical suffering and death is the least of their worries. Unless they repent and commit themselves to Jesus, an eternity in hell awaits.

Now's the time to be ready. Now's the time to help others understand the urgency.

Day 85

And the beast was allowed to wage war against God's holy people and to conquer them. And he was given authority to rule over every tribe and people and language and nation. And all the people who belong to this world worshiped the beast. They are the ones whose names were not written in the Book of Life that belongs to the Lamb who was slaughtered before the world was made (Revelation 13:7-8).

The Beast, or Antichrist, under the authority of the dragon, Satan, will *rule over every tribe and people and language and nation*. All the world will worship him.

Once again, we see why this Beast is called the Antichrist. He's a lying copier of Jesus. While Jesus reaches out in love, the Antichrist reaches out in hatred. While Jesus came to save, the Antichrist will come *to steal and kill and destroy* (John 10:10a).

In Revelation 5, we read about the song the saints sing to the Lamb of God: *[Y]our blood has ransomed people for God from every tribe and language and people and nation* (Revelation 5:9b). In today's passage, we read about the Antichrist ruling *over every tribe and people and language and nation*. While Jesus invites all people into his Kingdom as *joint-heirs* (Romans 8:17, BLB) and allows them the freedom to choose or reject him, the Antichrist forces his rule on all who remain on Planet Earth after the Rapture.

The only Christians on Earth after the Rapture will be: (1) non-Jews who put their faith in Jesus after the Rapture; and

(2) Jews who turned to Jesus after the Rapture. Both groups will be hunted. The Jews will be under God's special protection, but their lives will definitely not be easy. The non-Jews will be slaughtered.

Other than the two aforementioned groups, the whole world will worship Satan and the Antichrist. John identifies these people as *all the people who belong to this world*. As Jesus prayed to the Father before His crucifixion, He identified those who belonged to him: *They do not belong to this world any more than I do* (John 17:16). And Peter reminded us, those who belong to Jesus are merely *temporary residents and foreigners* (1 Peter 2:11a) on this Earth. This world is not our home.

As our passage today makes clear, those who choose to worship Satan and the Antichrist *are the ones whose names were not written in the Book of Life that belongs to the Lamb who was slaughtered before the world was made.*

Before the world was made, God's plan for our redemption was in place. The Father, Son, and Holy Spirit knew we would need a Savior, and Jesus, the One and Only Son of God, chose to suffer and die to pay our sin-debt. As Paul puts it: *When we were utterly helpless, Christ came at just the right time and died for us sinners* (Romans 5:6).

Speaking of *just the right time*, let me leave you with one last quote from the Apostle Paul: *Today is the day of salvation* (2 Corinthians 6:2). Don't put it off. Don't doubt. Be sure your name is *written in the Book of Life*.

Day 86

The Antichrist appears on the scene after the Rapture, *[a]nd all the people who belong to this world worshiped the beast. They are the ones whose names were not written in the Book of Life that belongs to the Lamb* (Revelation 13:7-8a).

Having seen what lies ahead for those who are left on Earth after the Rapture, John states a clear warning: *Anyone with ears to hear should listen and understand. Anyone who is destined for prison will be taken to prison. Anyone destined to die by the sword will die by the sword* (Revelation 13:9).

Nothing good awaits those left on Earth. *Anyone who is destined for prison will be taken to prison. Anyone destined to die by the sword will die by the sword.* Unless a person is already in heaven via death prior to the Rapture, or by having been taken from Earth in the Rapture, being left on Earth either means: (1) remaining lost and choosing to worship the Beast, the Antichrist; or, (2) turning to Jesus and refusing to worship the Beast. And turning to Jesus will result in being killed, whether by being sentenced to death in prison or by being hunted down and slaughtered elsewhere.

There's also a second meaning to that warning. Those who follow the Beast will be destined for the prison of eternal hell and, before that, will *die by the sword* right here on Earth.

Let me give you a little sneak preview of how this happens. John says in Revelation 19: *Then I saw heaven opened, and a white horse was standing there. Its rider was named Faithful and True, for he judges fairly and wages a righteous war. He wore a robe dipped in blood, and his title was the Word of*

God. From his mouth came a sharp sword to strike down the nations (verses 11, 13, 15a).

And in case there's still any doubt as to the identity of the *Faithful and True* rider, John goes on to tell us: *On his robe at his thigh was written this title: King of all kings and Lord of all lords* (Revelation 19:16). Jesus will lead his army and end the reign of Satan and the Antichrist.

Again, John stresses the urgency of genuine salvation: *This means that God's holy people must endure persecution patiently and remain faithful* (Revelation 13:10). Those who miss the Rapture and, afterwards, commit their hearts and lives to Jesus Christ will endure indescribable torment. Yet even they are expected to *endure ... and remain faithful*. If they, as well as believers in many countries today, can be faithful even in the face of such difficulties, surely we who have no idea what it's like to suffer persecution can consistently live out our faith.

As I said a few days ago, real salvation lasts. A person who is truly saved grows in the Spirit. Grows to be more like Jesus.

Are you a professing Christian? If so, let me ask you a question: if you were the only example of Christ another person ever saw, what would they think of Jesus?

Day 87

Then I saw another beast come up out of the earth. He had two horns like those of a lamb, but he spoke with the voice of a dragon. He exercised all the authority of the first beast. And he required all the earth and its people to worship the first beast, whose fatal wound had been healed. He did astounding miracles, even making fire flash down to earth from the sky while everyone was watching. And with all the miracles he was allowed to perform on behalf of the first beast, he deceived all the people who belong to this world (Revelation 13:11-14a).

The second beast we meet in today's passage is none other than the False Prophet, the third person of the unholy trinity: the Dragon (Satan), the Antichrist, and the False Prophet. As I said a couple of days ago, Satan is a lying copier of Jesus. Which is why the False Prophet looks as innocent as *a lamb*.

But don't let appearances fool you, because this False Prophet speaks *with the voice of a dragon*. Just as with the Antichrist, Satan is in control of the False Prophet. And what does this False Prophet do? He works with *all the authority of the first beast*. And it's this False Prophet who requires *all the earth and its people to worship the first beast*, the Antichrist, who, like himself, is merely a puppet of Satan.

As another example of Satan imitating Jesus, the False Prophet does *astounding miracles, even making fire flash down to earth from the sky*. And what did all this accomplish? *[H]e deceived all the people who belong to this world.*

Who belongs *to this world*? All those who worship the first Beast, or Antichrist. These are the people who'll have missed out on the Rapture.

Mankind was made for heaven, but a personal commitment to Christ is the only way to get there. Hebrews 13:14 puts it this way: *For we have no permanent city here, but we are longing for the city which is soon to be ours.* Don't miss that little word there: *soon.*

I was at my elderly Great Aunt Jocie's when I was a youngster and she was talking about her favorite subject: Jesus. From the little nightstand that stood between her bed and rocker, she picked up her worn old Bible, pressed it to her breast, walked over to her window, and looked out at the evening sky. "Sometimes," she said, "I get so excited I can't sleep, wondering if this will be the night the Lord comes and takes me home."

Like the writer of Hebrews, she was *longing for* her eternal home. How about you? Are you looking forward to seeing Jesus face-to-face or petrified at the thought?

Day 88

Yesterday we met the second beast, known as the False Prophet. He promotes the first beast, the Antichrist, and both take their orders from the dragon, who is Satan.

He ordered the people to make a great statue of the first beast, who was fatally wounded and then came back to life. He was then permitted to give life to this statue so that it could speak. Then the statue of the beast commanded that anyone refusing to worship it must die (Revelation 13:14b-15).

In the two beasts, the Antichrist and the False Prophet, we see both government and religion, a lethal combination when you mix in the dragon, Satan, who is the third person of the unholy trinity. The False Prophet has a statue of the Antichrist made—*He ordered the people to make a great statue of the first beast*—and the statue is enthroned in the place of worship.

While some think the statue may be supernaturally animated—*it could speak*—the technology available today could easily create it. And note the first act of the statue: *Then the statue of the beast commanded that anyone refusing to worship it must die.*

How does the whole world see this and know this? Instant communication just like we have today. I can text a friend or family member anywhere in the world and ask a question, and I'll usually get a response within seconds. We are saturated with means of instant communication. This *statue of the beast* will be seen and known by everyone who remains on Earth during the Tribulation. And he will demand to be worshiped. Or else.

He required everyone—small and great, rich and poor, free and slave—to be given a mark on the right hand or on the forehead. And no one could buy or sell anything without that mark (Revelation 13:16-17a).

This passage introduces us to what is known as the Mark of the Beast. You've probably heard of the microchips that can be placed under your pet's skin in order to keep track of it in case your pet is ever lost or stolen. It can track that pet's exact location. This **mark** could very well be something similar. Already some companies are putting microchips under their employees' skin so they don't have to worry about keeping up with I.D. badges or keys, etc. Those with authority to enter certain areas can unlock any necessary door or piece of equipment simply by placing their microchip within range of the installed scanners at the work facility.

This same technology is also being considered for other purposes. Instead of worrying about carrying cash or a debit card, you simply scan your microchip at checkout when you buy groceries or clothes or anything else. Credit check to buy a car or a house? No problem. Scan the microchip and they'll know everything about you, from previous addresses to education and work history to every penny you have in the bank or elsewhere.

So, when it comes down to that or whatever other form of **mark** the Tribulation's unholy trinity brings into being, not one person on Earth will be able to work or buy or sell or access what funds they already have unless they have that **mark**.

Dear friends, be certain you won't be left behind. The winning side is that of the Lord Jesus. Christians won't be left here to suffer the Tribulation. Urge everyone you know to trust Jesus now.

Day 89

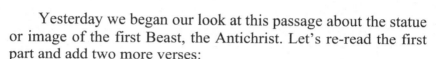

Yesterday we began our look at this passage about the statue or image of the first Beast, the Antichrist. Let's re-read the first part and add two more verses:

The False Prophet, who appeared as the second Beast, *ordered the people to make a great statue of the first beast ....* *He was then permitted to give life to this statue so that it could* *speak. Then the statue of the beast commanded that anyone* *refusing to worship it must die. He required everyone—small* *and great, rich and poor, free and slave—to be given a mark on* *the right hand or on the forehead. And no one could buy or sell* *anything without that mark, which was either the name of the* *beast or the number representing his name. Wisdom is needed* *here. Let the one with understanding solve the meaning of the* *number of the beast, for it is the number of a man. His number* *is 666* (Revelation 13:14b-18).

The use of the word *beast* for both the Antichrist and the False Prophet can get confusing, but just remember: the first Beast is the Antichrist; the second is the False Prophet. The False Prophet sees to it that the statue of the Antichrist is made and installed in the place of worship. And then the statue or image itself (*it could* *speak*) demanded to be worshiped by every person on Earth. He also required his *mark* of ownership to be placed on every person.

Here we see yet another example of Satan's imitation of Christ. If you look back at Revelation 7, we read where John *saw* *another angel coming up from the east, carrying the seal of the* *living God. And he shouted to those four angels, who had been* *given power to harm land and sea, 'Wait! Don't harm the land*

179

or the sea or the trees until we have placed the seal of God on the foreheads of his servants' (verses 2-3). While the Lord places His seal of ownership on those He has specially protected, the unholy trinity places the Antichrist's seal of ownership on those who worship the image of the Antichrist.

And what about this number 666? I don't begin to understand what it means. There are countless theories on its meaning. Suffice it to say that numbers in the Bible have significant meaning and this one clearly does. But how to understand it is beyond me. The important thing to take from this passage is that *it is the number of a man*. A specific man. A person who will appear as the Antichrist.

Today we see TV shows and movies and read fiction books that use the number 666 as part of some evil event or person. Fact is, the Antichrist isn't going to show up acting like some scary monster. Why would anyone want to follow someone like that? No, his true colors won't be seen until he's in power. And then, for those who've accepted his ownership by taking his mark, the time to repent will be past. Too late.

How many people do you know among you family and friends who don't know Jesus as Lord and Savior? What are you doing to point them to him?

Day 90

Referring to the first Beast, who is the Antichrist and the one whose talking statue or image is set up in the place of worship, John says: *Wisdom is needed here. Let the one with understanding solve the meaning of the number of the beast, for it is the number of a man. His number is 666* (Revelation 13:18).

The first beast, or the Antichrist, is clearly a man. But understanding the meaning of the number 666 is a futile effort. We don't need to get hung up on trying to figure out what it means.

Now let's take a look at some far more encouraging news: *Then I saw the Lamb standing on Mount Zion, and with him were 144,000 who had his name and his Father's name written on their foreheads* (Revelation 14:1).

Who are these 144,000? Jews saved during the Tribulation and marked by God with a protective seal: *And I heard how many were marked with the seal of God—144,000 were sealed from all the tribes of Israel* (Revelation 7:4).

The Lamb of God is seen *standing on Mount Zion* with the 144,000 Jewish believers redeemed during the Tribulation. Jerusalem is referred to as *Mount Zion* in many passages throughout the Bible and it's to this place the Lord will bring the 144,000 specially protected Jews. Centuries earlier, the prophet Joel spoke of this time: *But everyone who calls on the name of the Lord will be saved, for some on Mount Zion in Jerusalem will escape, just as the Lord has said. These will be among the survivors whom the Lord has called* (Joel 2:32).

And I heard a sound from heaven like the roar of mighty ocean waves or the rolling of loud thunder. It was like the sound of many harpists playing together. This great choir sang a wonderful new song in front of the throne of God and before the four living beings and the twenty-four elders. No one could learn this song except the 144,000 who had been redeemed from the earth (Revelation 14:2-3).

The Lord's voice roars like the sound of *mighty ocean waves or ... loud thunder*. And who are the *many harpists*? Revelation 5:8b has already shown us that *the four living beings and the twenty-four elders fell down before the Lamb. Each one had a harp*. In today's passage, John says the choir sounded like *many harpists playing together*, but, actually, the choir itself is singing in perfect harmony with the accompanying harpists.

"This great choir sang a wonderful new song in front of the throne of God. The 144,000 are on Mount Zion, but, in their spirits, their joyful worship transports them to the very *throne of God*. This is what true, passionate worship can do.

When was the last time your praise and worship took you to the very *throne of God*?

Revelation 14

Day 91

Referring to the 144,000 standing on Mount Zion with the Lord, John says: *They have kept themselves as pure as virgins, following the Lamb wherever He goes. They have been purchased from among the people on the earth as a special offering to God and to the Lamb. They have told no lies; they are without blame* (Revelation 14:4-5).

Here again, we're looking at the 144,000 Jewish believers who have been saved during the Tribulation. Are they truly *virgins*? Possibly, but we also have to consider passages like Jeremiah 14:17 where the Lord calls Israel *my virgin daughter— my precious people*. And in Lamentations 2:13, God calls them his *Virgin Daughter Zion* (NIV).

Whether the virginity of the 144,000 is literal or spiritual, we know for sure that these are faithful believers *following the Lamb wherever He goes*. We also know *[t]hey have been purchased from among the people on the earth.* No matter how far the Jewish people have been scattered across the world, the Lord knows every one of them and his Holy Spirit calls to each of them.

Many Bible scholars believe, and I agree, that those who turn to Christ during the Tribulation will do so early on. The Antichrist isn't going to leave alive any believer he can get his hands on, so even though the slaughter will be great, those who die refusing to give their allegiance to the Antichrist will spend eternity with Jesus.

They have told no lies; they are without blame. There are no perfect people. Even though John says these people ***have kept themselves as pure as virgins***, I believe this is a statement about God's total forgiveness, the wiping away of every wrongdoing ever committed by any of the 144,000.

These Jewish believers will also have turned to Christ early in the days of the Tribulation. But unlike the non-Jews, these people are ***a special offering to God and to the Lamb***, in that they will have God's seal protecting them and they will very likely be instrumental in turning many other people to Jesus as they endure the hardships of the Tribulation. This is why they are seen as standing and singing before God's throne.

Hopefully no one reading this will wait until after the Rapture to turn to Jesus, but for every person who puts their faith in him before the Rapture or even after the horrors of the Tribulation begin, Paul makes this wonderful promise: ***He has brought you into his own presence, and you are holy and blameless as you stand before him without a single fault*** (Colossians 1:22b).

Jesus paid it all. It's that simple, folks. What we couldn't do for our sorry ol' selves, Jesus did for us. He paid our sin-debt as the Only Perfect Sacrifice. Through the precious blood of Jesus, any person who has committed their heart and life to him can stand before the throne ***holy and blameless ... without a single fault***.

Knowing everything he's forgiven me, that, my friends, is a miracle. I know I'm a long way from where I need to be, but I want to show my love and gratitude by living a life that honors and serves him. How about you?

Day 92

And I saw another angel flying through the sky, carrying the eternal Good News to proclaim to the people who belong to this world—to every nation, tribe, language, and people. 'Fear God,' he shouted. 'Give glory to him. For the time has come when he will sit as judge. Worship him who made the heavens, the earth, the sea, and all the springs of water (Revelation 14:6-7).

There will come a time when every person on Earth worships Jesus Christ. Paul, speaking of Jesus, tells us in Philippians 2:9-11: ***God elevated him to the place of highest honor and gave him the name above all other names, that at the name of Jesus every knee should bow, in heaven and on earth and under the earth, and every tongue declare that Jesus Christ is Lord, to the glory of God the Father.*** It's not a matter of *if* a person will bow and confess Jesus as Lord; it's a matter of *when*.

But in today's passage we see an angel preaching the Gospel! This is the only place in the New Testament where you'll see this happening. Why? Because this is a special angel on special assignment during the Tribulation.

It's we humans who are given the privilege and responsibility of sharing the ***eternal Good News***. Jesus himself commanded us to ***go and make disciples*** (Matthew 28:19a). We're not to wait on the preacher, or our Bible study teacher, or even an angel, to do it for us. Spreading the ***eternal Good News*** is the job of every believer.

Who does this angel's message reach? *[E]very nation, tribe, language, and people.* Jesus told his disciples in Matthew 24:14 that *the Good News about the Kingdom will be preached throughout the whole world, so that all nations will hear it; and then the end will come.*

Nothing unclear about that statement, is there? While it's every believer's job to get the Word out, the Lord will even appoint an angel to announce his message worldwide so all are *without excuse* (Romans 1:20b, NIV) if they reject Christ's free offer of salvation.

When will this angel make his announcement? As I've said all along, the timeline of the events John records in the Revelation isn't necessarily in order. Based on the verses that follow the first angel's warning, it seems likely that this occurs at or near the beginning of the Tribulation. Why do I say this? Because in just a few more verses, we read: *Here is a call for the endurance of the saints who keep the commandments of God and the faith of Jesus. And I heard a voice from heaven telling me to write, 'Blessed are the dead—those who die in the Lord from this moment on'* (Revelation 14:12-13).

The angel's warning is dire: *For the time has come when he will sit as judge.* Time is running out and those who wait until after the Rapture of the Church will be left to suffer tremendously for their refusal to worship the Antichrist, or Beast. As Verse 13 makes evident, during the Tribulation, physical death will be far preferable to life on Earth for those who truly know the Lord.

The Rapture could occur at any second. Make sure you know Jesus. Do your part to point others to him. Speak the truth in love.

Day 93

In Revelation 14, we meet three angels, the first of whom we saw yesterday as he carried *the eternal Good News* (Revelation 14:6a) as a dire warning *to every nation, tribe, language, and people. 'Fear God,' he shouted. 'Give glory to him. For the time has come when he will sit as judge* (Revelation 14:6b-7a).

This is a special angel on special assignment during the Tribulation. Regardless of the pressure to worship the Antichrist, this angel's worldwide message means all people remaining on the Earth after the Rapture are *without excuse* (Romans 1:20b, NIV) if they reject Christ's free offer of salvation.

Then a second angel followed, saying, 'Fallen, fallen is Babylon the great, who has made all the nations drink the wine of the passion of her immorality' (Revelation 14:8).

Babylon is synonymous with evil, but, in this case, rather than pointing to a specific city, this is likely a reference to the false religion and political realm of the Antichrist. In spite of God's warnings, including that of the first angel we saw in today's passage, the nations will have followed in the immoral, sacrilegious practices led by the Antichrist and his False Prophet. We'll learn more about Babylon in Chapter 17.

And a third angel followed them, calling out in a loud voice, 'If anyone worships the beast and its image, and receives its mark on his forehead or on his hand, he too will drink the wine of God's anger, poured undiluted into the cup of his wrath. And he will be tormented in fire and brimstone in the presence of the holy angels and of the Lamb. And the smoke of their torment will rise forever and ever. Day and night there will be no rest for those who worship the beast and its image, or for anyone who receives the mark of its name' (Revelation 14:9-11).

First, let me stop here and say that no one will "accidentally" take the Mark of the Beast. Some people worry about the things that have already been mentioned, like microchips under the skin that could end up being the Mark of the Beast. No one will be forced to take the mark. No one will be tricked into taking the mark. No one has to worry about the mark unless they're still here after the Church has been taken into glory.

But for those who do accept the Mark of the Beast—which means declaring their allegiance to the Antichrist—they, along with Satan and all his followers, will *drink the wine of God's anger*. And John makes it clear that it will not be tempered with any compassion whatsoever. *[T]he wine of God's anger* will be *poured undiluted into the cup of his wrath*.

When the Tribulation begins, anyone who accepts the Mark of the Beast is doomed. Forgiveness will no longer be offered. Any person who follows the Antichrist and his False Prophet *will be tormented in fire and brimstone …. And the smoke of their torment will rise forever and ever. Day and night there will be no rest for those who worship the beast and its image.*

I realize this is scary stuff and it's not good news, but the Good News is that those who have put their faith in Jesus Christ won't be here to experience any of it. We will be celebrating the Savior in glory.

Day 94

The third angel in Revelation 14 warns: *Anyone who worships the beast and his statue or who accepts his mark on the forehead or on the hand ... will be tormented with fire and burning sulfur ... and they will have no relief day or night* (Revelation 14:9b, 10b, 11b).

This means that God's holy people must endure persecution patiently, obeying his commands and maintaining their faith in Jesus (Revelation 14:12). Read verse 12 again. How do we learn to *endure ... patiently*? By (1) *obeying his commands* and (2) *maintaining ... faith in Jesus*.

Do you have a car? If you do, you know it requires maintenance. If you don't keep air in the tires, you won't be going anywhere. If you don't keep fuel in the tank, that car is going nowhere. Brakes? Yeah, they're kind of important too. And I could list a few jillion others things from oil to filters. The care you give your car will greatly determine how long and how well it can function as your transportation.

How about a body? If you're reading this, I'm betting you have one. And if you give it proper rest and a good nutritious diet and exercise, you stand a much better chance of keeping it healthy. You have to do your part to maintain it. The care you give your body will certainly affect how long and how well it can function as your earthly means of getting around.

Likewise, we must not only obey the Lord's commands, we must also do regular maintenance on our faith. We can't be people of the Word if we don't know the Word.

Remember taking tests in school? Your success reflected how much you studied and prepared. News flash: your faith is being tested right now, right here, every moment, every day. And your responses to whatever comes your way are wholly defined by how well you're read up, prayed up, and prepared. As long as you're breathing, your faith will be tested. Don't fail. Be ready.

For those who wait until after the Rapture to turn to Jesus, their faith is going to be their only hope. It's our only Hope too, and his name is Jesus. Tell somebody.

Day 95

And I heard a voice from heaven saying, 'Write this down: Blessed are those who die in the Lord from now on. Yes, says the Spirit, they are blessed indeed, for they will rest from their hard work; for their good deeds follow them!' (Revelation 14:13).

Martyrs of the Rapture are going to be the happiest celebrants when they get to glory. They will be *blessed indeed, for they will rest from their hard work.* I can't begin to fathom what these people will have to do to survive for any length of time during the Tribulation. Neither can I comprehend the urgency they will feel to let others know how wrong they'd been by not believing in Jesus sooner.

Hmmm. Why can't I comprehend the urgency? Because I can't even wrap my head around how urgent it is to warn people right now. Sad but true, people die unexpectedly every day. And for those who die not knowing Jesus, their eternal fate is a terrible one. We need to do everything we can to make sure people understand there are only two choices: heaven or hell; Jesus or Satan.

After John sees the three angels introduced to us at the beginning of Revelation 14, John sees *a white cloud, and seated on the cloud was someone like the Son of Man. He had a gold crown on his head and a sharp sickle in his hand* (Revelation 14:14).

This figure John sees is: (1) seated on a white cloud; (2) wearing a gold crown; and (3) holding *a sharp sickle in his hand.*

This can only be Jesus Christ, and he is ready to render justice upon the Earth.

Then another angel came from the Temple and shouted to the one sitting on the cloud, 'Swing the sickle, for the time of harvest has come; the crop on earth is ripe.' So the one sitting on the cloud swung his sickle over the earth, and the whole earth was harvested" (Revelation 14:15-16).

This passage can be really confusing since an angel is heard telling Jesus: *Swing the sickle.* This angel most assuredly isn't ordering Jesus to do anything. He's merely affirming what the Lord is about to do.

Just to give you a heads-up, in addition to the sickle held by the Lord's own hand, we're going to see an angel holding another sickle, plus another angel who comes from the heavenly altar. I'll save all that for tomorrow, but, for now, note the latter half of verse 15: *the time of harvest has come; the crop on earth is ripe."*

That word translated *ripe* actually means overripe. I don't think it'd be a stretch to even define it as putrid. Stinking. Rotten. Well overdue for harvest. In other words, the Lord has been more than patient with this stinkin', rotten, evil world, but time's up.

[A]nd after that comes judgment (Hebrews 9:27b) at the Great White Throne of God, the place of final judgment for *anyone whose name was not found recorded in the Book of Life* (Revelation 20:15a).

Warn your friends. Warn your family. You want all their names in the Lamb's Book of Life.

Day 96

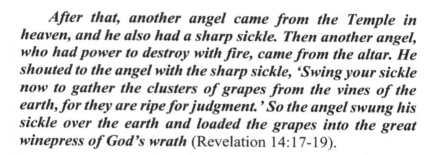

After that, another angel came from the Temple in heaven, and he also had a sharp sickle. Then another angel, who had power to destroy with fire, came from the altar. He shouted to the angel with the sharp sickle, 'Swing your sickle now to gather the clusters of grapes from the vines of the earth, for they are ripe for judgment.' So the angel swung his sickle over the earth and loaded the grapes into the great winepress of God's wrath (Revelation 14:17-19).

In addition to the sickle held by the Lord's own hand, there's also an angel holding a sickle plus another angel who *came from the altar*. Who is this angel who *came from the altar*? It's quite possibly the angel we saw in Revelation 8: *Then another angel with a gold incense burner came and stood at the altar. And a great amount of incense was given to him to mix with the prayers of God's people as an offering on the gold altar before the throne. Then the angel filled the incense burner with fire from the altar and threw it down upon the earth; and thunder crashed, lightning flashed, and there was a terrible earthquake* (verses 3 and 5).

Note the incense the angel carries is mixed *with the prayers of God's people*. What prayers? In this instance, we need to look back at Revelation 6: *I saw under the altar the souls of all who had been martyred for the word of God and for being faithful in their testimony. They shouted to the Lord and said, 'O Sovereign Lord, holy and true, how long before you judge the people who belong to this world and avenge our blood for what they have*

193

done to us?' Then a white robe was given to each of them. And they were told to rest a little longer until the full number of their brothers and sisters—their fellow servants of Jesus who were to be martyred—had joined them (Verses 9b-11).

The first of the Tribulation martyrs are seen **under the altar**. Why there? An altar symbolizes both sacrifice and worship, and these believers are covered by the blood. They may have waited until the eleventh hour to put their faith in Jesus, but they did turn to him and refused to deny him even at the cost of their earthly lives.

So, in response to the prayers of these martyred souls and following the lead of the Lord Jesus, *the angel swung his sickle over the earth and loaded the grapes into the great winepress of God's wrath.*

The all-out, undiluted wrath of God is unthinkable. After all the years the Lord tempered his responses with grace and mercy, the Earth is now *ripe for judgment*. And as we saw yesterday, that word *ripe* really means overripe, as in far overdue. God's patience with disobedient man has run out and no unbeliever can escape the fury the Lord is unleashing.

I hope you're doing more than reading through these. Study the Word. Know it for yourself. And share it with others while there's still time.

Day 97

John sees *the great winepress of God's wrath* (Revelation 14:19b) as it's being filled with those who have rejected Christ as Lord and Savior. These people—figuratively referred to here as *grapes—were trampled in the winepress outside the city, and blood flowed from the winepress in a stream about 180 miles long and as high as a horse's bridle* (Revelation 14:20).

Armageddon. The final battleground before the Millennial Reign of Christ. This battlefield around Jerusalem will cover 180 miles, a distance that had to be mindboggling to John since covering that many miles would have taken weeks in his day. And in this vision, John sees more blood, more slaughter than he could even describe. We'll learn more about Armageddon later.

Then I saw in heaven another marvelous event of great significance. Seven angels were holding the seven last plagues, which would bring God's wrath to completion. I saw before me what seemed to be a glass sea mixed with fire. And on it stood all the people who had been victorious over the beast and his statue and the number representing his name (Revelation 15:1-2a).

Again, let me remind you that the events we read about in the Revelation are not necessarily in chronological order. John has mentioned the upcoming Battle of Armageddon and now he's telling about the *last plagues, which would bring God's wrath to completion*. John is filling in more detail on what's to come.

I saw before me what seemed to be a glass sea mixed with fire. And on it stood all the people who had been victorious over the beast and his statue and the number representing his name.

John has shown us what would take place on Earth as holy wrath is unleashed upon those who have rejected the Lord Jesus. Now he shows us the preparation going on in heaven before the Battle of Armageddon. As the seven angels hold the seven plagues to be poured out onto the Earth, John also sees *the people who had been victorious over the beast and his statue and the number representing his name*.

These martyrs, whom I believe are the same Tribulation martyrs we saw earlier beneath the altar of the Lord, are now standing on a sea of glass, just as described in Revelation 4:6a: *In front of the throne was a shiny sea of glass, sparkling like crystal.*

We can speculate until the cows come home about the significance of John's description of *a glass sea mixed with fire*, but let me just throw out two probabilities: (1) The fire could represent the purifying process these martyrs went through during their fiery trials; or (2) it could represent the purifying fire of the Holy Spirit. Either way, I believe it's an indicator of the absolute purity of these people.

When you've given up all earthly things, including your very lives, because of your faith and trust in Jesus Christ, you've been through the fire. You're pure. You're holy. And you're robed in the righteousness of Christ. Let's not forget that the finest Christian who ever lived didn't get to heaven on his or her own merit, but strictly because of Jesus Christ's completed work of salvation. As Isaiah 64:6b reminds us, *our righteous deeds ... are nothing but filthy rags*.

We'll learn more about this group of Tribulation martyrs tomorrow. For now, let me leave you with this thought: they're standing directly before the throne of God and they aren't afraid. They're rejoicing. They have nothing to hide, nothing to be ashamed of. They've given their all for Jesus. May all of us be willing to do the same.

Revelation 15

Day 98

Yesterday John told us about the *[s]even angels ... holding the seven last plagues* (Revelation 15:1b) and about the glass sea upon which *stood all the people who had been victorious over the beast and his statue and the number representing his name* (Revelation 15:2b). These are apparently the same Tribulation martyrs we saw earlier in the Book of Revelation beneath the altar of the Lord, but they are now standing on a sea of glass as described in Revelation 4:6a: *In front of the throne was a shiny sea of glass, sparkling like crystal.*

Back to Chapter 15: *They were all holding harps that God had given them. And they were singing the song of Moses, the servant of God, and the song of the Lamb: 'Great and marvelous are your works, O Lord God, the Almighty. Just and true are your ways, O King of the nations. Who will not fear you, Lord, and glorify your name? For you alone are holy. All nations will come and worship before you, for your righteous deeds have been revealed* (Revelation 15:2c-4).

The only other people we see in heaven who are holding or playing harps are the 24 elders (see Revelation 5:8), so these must be the harpists we hear accompanying the singing of the 144,000 in Revelation 14:2. Here, we see every Tribulation martyr has their own harp, but unlike the 144,000 who were given their own special song of praise—*No one could learn this song except the 144,000* (Revelation 14:3b)—these martyrs are *singing the song of Moses, the servant of God, and the song of the Lamb*. And as we've seen, John wrote down the words of the song. These Tribulation martyrs are given the privileges of: (1) standing on the sea of glass before the throne of God; (2) playing harps just like the 24 elders; and (3) singing the song of Moses and of the Lamb.

In Matthew 20, we read Jesus' Parable of the Vineyard Workers. Jesus begins by saying, ***The Kingdom of Heaven is like the landowner who went out early one morning to hire workers for his vineyard*** (Matthew 20:1). Problem is, some were hired at the start of the workday, others at midday, some in late afternoon, and others pretty close to quitting time. And yet every last one of them received a full day's wages. Doesn't seem fair, does it? Yet, as the landowner points out to the workers who complained, ***Friend, I haven't been unfair! Didn't you agree to work all day for the usual wage? I wanted to pay this last worker the same as you*** (Revelation 20:13, 14b).

The day you accepted Jesus Christ as Lord and Savior, you committed to work in the Kingdom. Whether you've been doing that for half a century or are just getting started, your job assignment began the moment you said, "Yes" to Jesus' invitation of salvation. And every person—latecomer or not—receives a place in heaven.

If you read that entire parable, you won't see any info about what sort of workers these were, but in spite of that, we can be sure that, for whatever amount of time those workers were put out into the field, they were busy. They were doing what they were told to do. They were working. Otherwise, Jesus wouldn't have called them ***workers***. We, my friends, aren't workers if we're idle. We're idlers. And that's not what Jesus called us to be. He said we're to *[w]ork hard to enter the narrow door to God's Kingdom* (Matthew 13:24a). No, your works don't get you into heaven, but, depending on your service for the Kingdom, there are rewards you'll receive or miss out on once you get there. Your works are also evidence of a genuine conversion experience. If you've given your heart and life to Christ, he's who you're serving. He's who you're honoring in your walk and talk. And he is who has paid for your home in heaven.

Day 99

John now moves from the joyful scene of the martyrs in heaven to the work of the *seven angels ... holding the seven last plagues* (Revelation 15:1b).

Then I looked and saw that the Temple in heaven, God's Tabernacle, was thrown wide open. The seven angels who were holding the seven plagues came out of the Temple. They were clothed in spotless white linen with gold sashes across their chests. Then one of the four living beings handed each of the seven angels a gold bowl filled with the wrath of God, who lives forever and ever. The Temple was filled with smoke from God's glory and power. No one could enter the Temple until the seven angels had completed pouring out the seven plagues (Revelation 15:5-8).

In Revelation 8, we were introduced to seven angels with trumpets. Are these the same angels? I don't know, but my guess is, yes. However, the judgment we're going to see in Revelation 16 isn't the same as that of Revelation 8. While Revelation 8's devastation is partial, what we'll see in Chapter 16 is absolute. As I keep reminding us, the imagery in the Book of Revelation can be confusing, but hang with me and we'll grow to understand more and more.

The seven angels who were holding the seven plagues came out of the Temple. They were clothed in spotless white linen. Look where these angels came from: the Temple. Not an earthly one, but the Temple in heaven. Is this a physical temple? Again, I don't know, which I've already admitted and will continue to say a lot. What I do know is that in the New Jerusalem, John tells us:

I saw no temple in the city, for the Lord God Almighty and the Lamb are its temple (Revelation 21:22).

Any way we slice it, we can say one thing for sure: these seven angels are coming from the presence of God, and *[t]he Temple was filled with smoke from God's glory and power*. Not the angels' *glory and power*. God's, and God's alone. Just as we see in Isaiah 6 and 2 Chronicles 5, as well as a number of other places, the Shekinah glory of God overwhelms everyone in his presence.

Here's a good spot to note that these angels may be mighty, but they're operating in the power and authority of the Lord. We don't pray to angels. We don't command angels. Holy angels obey God and do his will, not ours.

No one could enter the Temple until the seven angels had completed pouring out the seven plagues (Revelation 15:8b). Don't skate over this passage, because it's enormously significant. To enter the Temple was to come into the presence of Almighty God. Here, we see access to the presence of God halted. In other words, the time for repentance is past and the time of final judgment is at hand. Jesus' work as our Mediator is finished and he is now the Judge of disobedient man.

If we can only share the smallest inkling of this with those who don't know Jesus, we'll have planted seeds before the time of harvest. And the harvest is close. So close.

Revelation 16

Day 100

Yesterday we saw the *[s]even angels ... holding the seven last plagues* (Revelation 15:1b). The time has come for the Lord's judgment on the unrepentant of Earth to rain down in full force.

Then I heard a mighty voice from the Temple say to the seven angels, 'Go your ways and pour out on the earth the seven bowls containing God's wrath.' So the first angel left the Temple and poured out his bowl on the earth, and horrible, malignant sores broke out on everyone who had the mark of the beast and who worshiped his statue (Revelation 16:1-2).

First, who is this *mighty voice* speaking *from the Temple*? Since we've already seen that *[n]o one could enter the Temple until the seven angels had completed pouring out the seven plagues* (Revelation 15:8b), the only possible answer is the Lord himself.

When this first angel pours onto the Earth his bowl *containing God's wrath*, John sees that *horrible, malignant sores broke out on everyone who had the mark of the beast and who worshiped his statue*. Speculation about what causes these sores include nuclear fallout and a host of other possibilities. Suffice it to say that, by whatever means he chooses, God himself marks these people with *horrible, malignant sores*.

Then the second angel poured out his bowl on the sea, and it became like the blood of a corpse. And everything in the sea died (Revelation 16:3). Let me remind us again that while we see angels with trumpets rendering God's judgment in Revelation 8, that devastation is partial. What we see here in Chapter 16 is total: *[E]verything in the sea died* and the water *became like the blood of a corpse* (Revelation 16:3).

Then the third angel poured out his bowl on the rivers and springs, and they became blood (Revelation 16:4). Real blood? Maybe, maybe not. God can do whatever He chooses. What we can know with certainty is that the people of Earth are now without any source of water. First the sea waters and then the freshwater springs and rivers have thickened *like the blood of a corpse*. And no one can survive for any significant length of time without water. These judgments must be happening at or toward the very end of the seven years of Tribulation.

As horrific as what takes place when these first three angels pour out their bowls of God's wrath upon the Earth, what follows is terrifying enough to almost defy description. And such is the fate of every person remaining on Earth who has rejected the Lord Jesus Christ's free offer of salvation.

Terror upon terror, horror upon horror is coming. And the only way to miss out is to surrender to God through faith in Jesus Christ before the Church is taken out of this world and the Tribulation begins.

Day 101

We've begun our look at the seven angels of Revelation 15. In Revelation 16 they begin pouring out the bowls of God's undiluted wrath on the Earth. When this first angel pours his bowl onto the Earth, *horrible, malignant sores broke out on everyone who had the mark of the beast and who worshiped his statue* (Revelation 16:2b).

Then the second angel poured out his bowl on the sea, and it became like the blood of a corpse. And everything in the sea died. Then the third angel poured out his bowl on the rivers and springs, and they became blood (Revelation 16:3-4). The people of Earth are now without any source of water, which means their survival time will be very short.

And I heard the angel who had authority over all water saying, 'You are just, O Holy One, who is and who always was, because you have sent these judgments. Since they shed the blood of your holy people and your prophets, you have given them blood to drink. It is their just reward.' And I heard a voice from the altar, saying, 'Yes, O Lord God, the Almighty, your judgments are true and just' (Revelation 16:5-7).

In these last three verses, we hear two voices: the voice of *the angel who had authority over all water* and *a voice from the altar*. The first voice is identified as that of an angel, but he is never named. As I've said before, angels may be powerful, but they are working in and through the power of God. We aren't to worship them or pray to them. They are God's servants doing God's will.

The second voice comes from the heavenly altar. Who is this? Possibly one or all of the cherubim, the four living beings we read about in Revelation 4, since they are continually encircling the throne of God.

What's happening to the Earth and its inhabitants shouldn't have taken anyone by surprise. After all, the Lord gave them warning after warning through his Word, through his Holy Spirit's calling, and through his faithful children who obey his command to *[g]o and make disciples* (Matthew 28:19a). And yet here these people are, lost and with no hope of redemption.

How about you? Are you an obedient child of God? Are you telling others about Jesus? Are you working to bring others into the Kingdom? How many people will be in heaven because of your witness?

Day 102

A quick recap of the first three of the seven angels' bowls of God's wrath: When the first angel pours his bowl onto the Earth, the people become covered in cancerous sores. The second angel's bowl turns the Earth's bodies of saltwater to blood, and the third angel's bowl turns the fresh waters to blood. And there are four more bowls of God's undiluted holy wrath to be poured out.

Then the fourth angel poured out his bowl on the sun, causing it to scorch everyone with its fire. Everyone was burned by this blast of heat, and they cursed the name of God, who had control over all these plagues. They did not repent of their sins and turn to God and give him glory (Revelation 16:8-9).

This cataclysmic event may occur as the result of changes in the solar system or nuclear war. Who knows? Whatever sets it off, God is the Author, and as horrible as all of this will be, he will be cleansing the Earth of evil after having given people more than ample time to repent and turn to him.

And look at the people's reaction to these horrors: no remorse, no repentance. Just hatred. Even cursing God. There are no atheists at this point. Every lost soul on Earth knows *who had control over all these plagues*. Still, they refused to *repent of their sins and turn to God and give him glory*.

Many people believe God exists. A lot of people even acknowledge that Jesus is God. But those same people may only want God in their lives on their own terms to do their own bidding. God is no puppet. No human can boss God around. And for him to be anything less than Lord and Savior in a person's life is for that person to be merely aware of him but not belong to him.

Romans 10:9 makes it clear that true salvation includes two things: confession and repentance. *[I]f you confess with your mouth that Jesus is Lord and believe in your heart that God raised him from the dead, you will be saved* (ESV). And that's the only way anyone will be saved. Good works won't save you. Acknowledging the existence of God won't save you. Even believing Jesus is God won't save you unless you not only admit that, but also believe it in your heart.

Three more bowls of God's wrath to go and things only get worse for those who rejected Christ's offer of salvation.

Day 103

We've seen the results of the first four of the seven angels' bowls of God's wrath: cancerous sores all over the people; all the seas' waters coagulated into an undrinkable ooze like the blood of a dead man; followed by the same thing happening to all the freshwater rivers and streams. And then the sun becomes so hot that it burns the inhabitants of Earth with fire.

Then the fifth angel poured out his bowl on the throne of the beast, and his kingdom was plunged into darkness. His subjects ground their teeth in anguish, and they cursed the God of heaven for their pains and sores. But they did not repent of their evil deeds and turn to God (Revelation 16:10-11).

After the scorching fire of the sun, did the sun burn out? Again, I don't know. Whatever happens when the fifth angel pours out his bowl, it plunges Earth into total darkness. Cancerous sores all over their bodies; no source of water; bodies burned by scorching heat; and now they're in complete darkness. Are there any manmade light sources? Are power grids still working? Generators in operation? Again, I don't know, but God is no longer providing any source of light in the world.

Think about that awful darkness for just a moment. As we saw earlier in this study, Jesus said in John 9:5: *[W]hile I am here in the world, I am the light of the world.* He also said of those who would believe in him: *You are the light of the world* (Matthew 5:14a). Jesus has removed his Holy Spirit from this world. The True Church has been raptured from the Earth, and a world without God can only go from bad to worse, which is exactly what happens.

Then the sixth angel poured out his bowl on the great Euphrates River, and it dried up so that the kings from the east could march their armies toward the west without hindrance. And I saw three evil spirits that looked like frogs leap from the mouths of the dragon, the beast, and the false prophet. They are demonic spirits who work miracles and go out to all the rulers of the world to gather them for battle against the Lord on that great judgment day of God the Almighty (Revelation 16:12-14).

Even the mightiest of rivers, ***the great Euphrates River***, has now gone from coagulated blood-like ooze to being dry ground. And across it come ***the kings from the east*** and ***their armies***. Who is this? We can speculate all day long: China? Japan? The list goes on. But regardless of this multitude's identity, they're being drawn westward by the ***three evil spirits ... from the mouths of the dragon, the beast, and the false prophet***.

And while this unholy trinity—the dragon, the Antichrist, and the False Prophet—bring these armies to do battle, who are they going to battle against? *[T]he Lord*.

When you fight against God, there can only be one victor. This is why Ephesians 6 reminds us we're in a battle. If you're on God's side, this Earth is your battlefield, not your home. Suit up and be prepared to defend what you believe.

Put on the whole armor of God, that you may be able to stand against the schemes of the devil (Ephesians 6:11, ESV).

Day 104

We've looked at the results of the first five of the seven angels' bowls of God's wrath: cancerous sores all over the people, and all the seas' waters as well as fresh waters coagulated into an undrinkable ooze. Then the sun becomes so hot that it burns the inhabitants of Earth with fire, and that is followed by utter darkness.

Then the sixth angel poured out his bowl on the great Euphrates River, and it dried up so that the kings from the east could march their armies toward the west without hindrance. And I saw three evil spirits that looked like frogs leap from the mouths of the dragon, the beast, and the false prophet. They are demonic spirits who work miracles and go out to all the rulers of the world to gather them for battle against the Lord on that great judgment day of God the Almighty (Revelation 16:12-14).

[T]he great Euphrates River goes from coagulated blood-like ooze to being dry ground. And across it come *the kings from the east* and *their armies*, drawn westward by the *three evil spirits ... from the mouths of the dragon, the beast, and the false prophet*.

As the sixth angel begins his task, Jesus speaks: *Look, I will come as unexpectedly as a thief! Blessed are all who are watching for me, who keep their clothing ready so they will not have to walk around naked and ashamed* (Revelation 16:15). The warning is given over and over. Jesus will call his Church out *unexpectedly*. That's why we are to watch and be ready.

[S]o they will not have to walk around naked and ashamed. In Matthew 22, Jesus tells the Parable of the Wedding Feast,

saying: ***The Kingdom of Heaven can be illustrated by the story of a king who prepared a great wedding feast for his son.... [W]hen the king came in to meet the guests, he noticed a man who wasn't wearing the proper clothes for a wedding. Then the king said to his aides, 'Bind his hands and feet and throw Him into the outer darkness, where there will be weeping and gnashing of teeth'*** (Matthew 22:2, 11, 13).

Wedding clothes were provided by the bridegroom and his family. If anyone was at the wedding without proper wedding garments, it was because he was uninvited and unwelcome. While every person will one day stand before the Lord, those who have put their faith in Jesus will be robed in the righteousness of Christ while those who have rejected his free offer of salvation will stand at the Great White Throne of Judgment ***naked and ashamed***.

To give us warning after warning and opportunity after opportunity, God assuredly loves us with a love greater than we can fathom. How do you show your love for him?

Day 105

As the sixth of the seven angels pours out his bowl onto the Earth, Jesus issues this warning: *Look, I will come as unexpectedly as a thief! Blessed are all who are watching for me, who keep their clothing ready so they will not have to walk around naked and ashamed* (Revelation 16:15).

Another reminder of what's to come. Another reminder that the only clothing we can wear in the presence of God are robes of righteousness, the righteousness of Christ given only to those who have received him as Savior and Lord.

What had happened when the sixth angel poured out his bowl? John saw *the kings from the east* preparing to *march their armies toward the west without hindrance. And I saw three evil spirits that looked like frogs leap from the mouths of the dragon, the beast, and the false prophet. They are demonic spirits who ... go out to all the rulers of the world to gather them for battle against the Lord on that great judgment day of God the Almighty"* (Revelation 16:12b-14).

And the demonic spirits gathered all the rulers and their armies to a place with the Hebrew name Armageddon (Revelation 16:16). The word "Armageddon" is derived from two Greek words: *Har* and *Megiddo*, meaning *Mount Megiddo*. Its root is a verb meaning to cut, invade, and expose. As you see that word "cut," think about John's description of Jesus in Revelation 1:16: *[A] sharp two-edged sword came from his mouth.*

Then there's the word "invade." John sees *all the rulers and their armies* gathered.

Lastly, there's "expose." We've already seen the exposure of those who reject Christ. But for those in the battle of Armageddon, the Antichrist and his False Prophet will be exposed for the losers they are, and those who follow them will be sentenced to the same fate as this evil duo.

Just exactly where is Megiddo? It's located in the Valley of Jezreel southeast of Haifa in northern Israel. The city of Megiddo had been a Canaanite city until ***Joshua and the Israelite armies defeated*** its king and many others ***on the west side of the Jordan*** (Joshua 12:7b), and gave it to the tribe of Manasseh as part of their inheritance in the Promised Land. (Read Joshua 12:7-24 to learn more.) Is this really where the Battle of Armageddon will be fought? I don't know. There are tons of speculation, but the Bible doesn't give us the specifics.

And we've yet to see what happens when the seventh angel pours out that final bowl of God's undiluted wrath onto the Earth. I'll save that for tomorrow, unless the Lord calls his Church out before then.

Day 106

Then the seventh angel poured out his bowl into the air. And a mighty shout came from the throne in the Temple, saying, 'It is finished!' Then the thunder crashed and rolled and lightning flashed. And a great earthquake struck—the worst since people were placed on the Earth. The great city of Babylon split into three sections, and the cities of many nations fell into heaps of rubble.

So God remembered all of Babylon's sins, and he made her drink the cup that was filled with the wine of his fierce wrath. And every island disappeared, and all the mountains were leveled. There was a terrible hailstorm, and hailstones weighing as much as seventy-five pounds fell from the sky onto the people below. They cursed God because of the terrible plague of the hailstorm (Revelation 16:17-21).

From the throne in the Temple, we hear the shout, *It is finished!* When Jesus cried from the cross, *It is finished!* (John 19:30), he opened the doorway to heaven for all who would put their faith in him. However, the announcement we see this time proclaims the end of God's patience. All the opportunities to repent have come and gone.

Despite all the horrible disasters that have already devastated the Earth, we see even more: the greatest earthquake in history, with many cities completely demolished and every island sinking into the ooze that had once been seas and rivers. Every mountain is flattened, and there's a hailstorm with stones as heavy as 75 pounds pommeling the Earth and its inhabitants.

The great city of Babylon split into three sections. Who is this Babylon? For now, let me remind you of what we read in Chapter 14: *Then a second angel followed, saying, 'Fallen, fallen is Babylon the great, who has made all the nations drink the wine of the passion of her immorality'* (Revelation 14:8).

Babylon is synonymous with evil, so this is likely a reference to the false religion and political realm of the Antichrist and his False Prophet. But surely this realm has a seat, a headquarters city. After all, we're told in today's passage that *[t]he great city of Babylon split into three sections.* We'll learn more about that in the upcoming chapters.

Meanwhile, look again at Revelation 14:8. The angel in that passage says *Babylon the great … has made all the nations drink the wine of the passion of her immorality.* But now we see the tables turned. God is making Babylon *drink the cup that was filled with the wine of his fierce wrath.* All these disasters, and what is the people's response? *They cursed God,* and now these people will follow their leader into eternal damnation.

Compare their fate with what David wrote about in Psalm 23:6: *Surely your goodness and unfailing love will pursue me all the days of my life, and I will live in the house of the Lord forever.* Doesn't seem like a hard choice to me. I choose Jesus. Do you?

Revelation 17

Day 107

Now that all seven bowls of God's full-force wrath have been poured out onto the Earth by the seven angels, one of those angels speaks to John. This is a long passage, but we need to first see it as a whole before breaking it into sections.

One of the seven angels who had poured out the seven bowls came over and spoke to me. 'Come with me,' he said, 'and I will show you the judgment that is going to come on the great prostitute, who rules over many waters. The kings of the world have committed adultery with her, and the people who belong to this world have been made drunk by the wine of her immorality.'

So the angel took me in the Spirit into the wilderness. There I saw a woman sitting on a scarlet beast that had seven heads and ten horns, and blasphemies against God were written all over it. The woman wore purple and scarlet clothing and beautiful jewelry made of gold and precious gems and pearls. In her hand she held a gold goblet full of obscenities and the impurities of her immorality. A mysterious name was written on her forehead: 'Babylon the Great, Mother of All Prostitutes and Obscenities in the World.' I could see that she was drunk— drunk with the blood of God's holy people who were witnesses for Jesus. I stared at her in complete amazement.

'Why are you so amazed?' the angel asked. 'I will tell you the mystery of this woman and of the beast with seven heads and

215

ten horns on which she sits. The beast you saw was once alive but isn't now. And yet he will soon come up out of the bottomless pit and go to eternal destruction. And the people who belong to this world, whose names were not written in the Book of Life before the world was made, will be amazed at the reappearance of this beast who had died.

This calls for a mind with understanding: The seven heads of the beast represent the seven hills where the woman rules. They also represent seven kings. Five kings have already fallen, the sixth now reigns, and the seventh is yet to come, but his reign will be brief" (Revelation 17:1-10).

Today we meet the ***woman sitting on a scarlet beast that had seven heads and ten horns***. What or who is this ***beast*** she's sitting on? It is the Antichrist we saw in Revelation 13:1a: ***Then I saw a beast rising up out of the sea. It had seven heads and ten horns, with ten crowns on its horns.*** This woman, also referred to as a "harlot" or ***prostitute***, represents the false, immoral religion spread over the Earth by the Antichrist and False Prophet.

This woman is described as having ***[a] mysterious name ... written on her forehead: 'Babylon the Great, Mother of All Prostitutes and Obscenities in the World.'*** And John says: ***[S]he was drunk ... with the blood of God's holy people who were witnesses for Jesus.***

If you think the world hates us now, the present-day attitude toward Christians pales in comparison with the hatred that will permeate the Earth after the Rapture. ***Babylon the Great***, the leaders and followers of the false religion that will spread across the Earth, will slaughter ***God's holy people who*** [are] ***witnesses for Jesus***.

Yet as horrible as their deaths will be, those who die believing in Jesus will be raised to life eternal. The only thing those who reject Jesus have ahead of them is an eternity of torment.

We're digging even deeper tomorrow. Pray and prepare.

Day 108

We read the first 10 verses of Revelation 17 yesterday. Today let's take one small segment at a time: *One of the seven angels who had poured out the seven bowls came over and spoke to me. 'Come with me,' he said, 'and I will show you the judgment that is going to come on the great prostitute, who rules over many waters. The kings of the world have committed adultery with her, and the people who belong to this world have been made drunk by the wine of her immorality'* (Revelation 17:1-2).

We know this woman, *the great prostitute*, is also referred to as *Babylon*, representing the false, immoral religion spread over the Earth by the Antichrist and False Prophet. The world religion during the Tribulation will be as pagan and evil as imaginable, and everyone, including all the world leaders, will participate in this abominable cult.

So the angel took me in the Spirit into the wilderness. There I saw a woman sitting on a scarlet beast that had seven heads and ten horns, and blasphemies against God were written all over it. The woman wore purple and scarlet clothing and beautiful jewelry made of gold and precious gems and pearls. In her hand she held a gold goblet full of obscenities and the impurities of her immorality. A mysterious name was written on her forehead: 'Babylon the Great, Mother of All Prostitutes and Obscenities in the World.' I could see that she was drunk— drunk with the blood of God's holy people who were witnesses for Jesus (Revelation 17:3-6a).

John sees this *woman sitting on a scarlet beast that had seven heads and ten horns*. She rides upon the back of the beast known as the Antichrist. As described in Revelation 13, this beast is a human being, a man who, along with the False Prophet, is completely under the control of Satan and doing his bidding to lead the entire Tribulation world into damnation. And the religion they offer is as alluring as the most beautiful, immoral woman anyone has ever laid eyes on.

Notice this woman is wearing *purple and scarlet clothing*. The dyes to produce these colors were rare and costly and typically only used on garments worn by rulers and the incredibly wealthy. Religion is ruling the day through the authority of the Antichrist and the False Prophet.

A mysterious name was written on her forehead: 'Babylon the Great, Mother of All Prostitutes and Obscenities in the World.' We're already living in a world where so much wrong is being called right and so much that's right is being called wrong. By the time of the Tribulation, that attitude won't be remotely sugar-coated—it'll be flaunted far more blatantly than we see today. This false religion will be so vile that the world will take pride in its *prostitutes and obscenities*.

I stared at her in complete amazement. 'Why are you so amazed?' the angel asked. 'I will tell you the mystery of this woman and of the beast with seven heads and ten horns on which she sits' (Revelation 17:6b-7). John is astounded, but the angel assures him that the vision will be explained.

The Book of Revelation isn't an easy one to understand, but it is understandable. No, we may not grasp every detail, but anyone who takes the time to read and study it will realize that the time of the Tribulation is on the horizon and today, right here, right now, is the time to get busy telling others what's ahead for those who reject the Savior.

We'll look at the angel's explanation tomorrow. Again, I ask you to pray for wisdom and understanding as we continue.

Day 109

We've just begun picking apart the first 10 verses of Chapter 17 and we've learned that the woman in this passage represents the false, immoral religion spread over the Earth by the Antichrist and False Prophet.

John was so shocked by what he was shown that he *stared at her in complete amazement* (Revelation 17:6b). But the angel explains: *This calls for a mind that has wisdom. The seven heads are seven mountains on which the woman sits. There are also seven kings. Five have fallen, one is, and the other has not yet come; but when he does come, he must remain for only a little while* (Revelation 17:9-10, BSB).

Several translations use the word "hills" rather than *mountains* when translating this passage from the original language. Fact is, the word should be *mountains*. Many people— Protestants, that is, for the most part—want to point their fingers at the Roman Catholic Church and claim this passage is referring to Rome, which is known as the City Built on Seven Hills, as the seat of the New World Order, the one-world government and religion of the Tribulation. I'm not about to point a finger at any denomination, and I hope you won't, either.

In Biblical imagery, mountains are often synonymous with governments or ruling powers. This is more likely the reference here, since the very next verse talks about *seven kings*, or world powers: *Five have fallen.* When John received this Revelation, five world powers had already come and gone: the Egyptian, Assyrian, Babylonian, Medo-Persian, and Greek Empires.

[O]ne is. The Roman Empire was in power when John was given the Revelation. As John tells us at the beginning, *I was exiled to the island of Patmos for preaching the word of God and for my testimony about Jesus* (Revelation 1:9b). The Emperor of Rome—most likely Domitian—is who sentenced John to Patmos.

[A]nd the other has not yet come; but when he does come, he must remain for only a little while. Whoever or whatever government comes into power or is in power at the beginning of the Tribulation won't be in that position for long before the Antichrist makes his appearance and takes over.

Frightening times. *The scarlet beast ... is the eighth king* (Revelation 17:11). We'll learn more about him tomorrow. Meanwhile, let me remind you that none of these terrors will affect *those who are in Christ Jesus* (Romans 8:1b, NIV).

Day 110

The seven heads are seven mountains on which the woman sits. There are also seven kings. Five have fallen, one is, and the other has not yet come; but when he does come, he must remain for only a little while (Revelation 17:9-10, BSB).

If you're still unsure of the explanation of the *seven kings*, please go back and re-read yesterday's study before reading today's.

The scarlet beast that was, but is no longer, is the eighth king. He is like the other seven, and he, too, is headed for destruction. The ten horns of the beast are ten kings who have not yet risen to power. They will be appointed to their kingdoms for one brief moment to reign with the beast. They will all agree to give him their power and authority. Together they will go to war against the Lamb (Revelation 17:11-14a).

If we go back to Revelation 13, we see where we were introduced to the beast who rose out of the sea. This beast is a man, the Antichrist, who is mortally wounded and yet survives. Thus, he *was, but is no longer*. This is the most confusing part of this passage. Either this is simply a statement about the Antichrist returning to life after his mortal wound, or it's identifying the seventh king—*is no longer*—as the same person who becomes the eighth king after his miraculous recovery from his fatal wound.

This person, the Antichrist, empowered by Satan, will be the final human ruler on the Earth, and he will use all his forces to oppose those who belong to the Lamb of God, Jesus Christ. The *ten kings* may be actual rulers around the globe or a confederation of nations, and the number 10 may be figurative rather than literal. Point is, though, whoever is involved will have a short-lived place of authority: *They will be appointed to their kingdoms for one brief moment to reign with the beast. They will all agree to give him their power and authority.* These *kings* will be mere puppet rulers under the thumb of the Antichrist.

And *[t]ogether they will go to war against the Lamb* (Revelation 17:14a). But here's the Good News: *[T]he Lamb will defeat them because He is Lord of all Lords and King of all Kings. And his called and chosen and faithful ones will be with him* (Revelation 17:14b).

If you know Jesus Christ as your personal Lord and Savior, you, my friend, are *called and chosen* and one of the *faithful ones who will be with him*. I say it often: the proof is in the living. If you truly know him, you serve him. Faithfully. Do you?

Day 111

We looked at this passage yesterday, but let's see this one verse again before we move on. Speaking of Satan, the Antichrist, and his followers, Revelation 17:14a says: *Together they will go to war against the Lamb, but the Lamb will defeat them because He is Lord of All Lords and King of All Kings.*

Then the angel said to me, 'The waters where the prostitute is ruling represent masses of people of every nation and language. The scarlet beast and his ten horns all hate the prostitute. They will strip her naked, eat her flesh, and burn her remains with fire (Revelation 17:15-16).

We know this woman, *the great prostitute* (Revelation 17:1), also called "Babylon," represents the immoral post-Tribulation religion. In today's passage we see that this false religion has become worldwide: *The waters where the prostitute is ruling represent masses of people of every nation and language.* How is it possible for the Antichrist and his False Prophet to be in charge of the entire world's governments? Government and religion are working together hand-in-hand.

The scarlet beast and his ten horns all hate the prostitute. They will strip her naked, eat her flesh, and burn her remains with fire. Remember the ten kings we saw yesterday? They're the *ten horns* seen here. And we know they have all agreed *to give him their power and authority* (Revelation 17:13). Him who? The Antichrist.

Once the Antichrist has achieved his goal of bringing the world together under one religion and one governmental power, he won't need religion anymore, so he'll show his true colors and do away with it. He, like Nebuchadnezzar in the Old Testament, will demand to be worshiped (see Daniel 3), and he won't tolerate any other form of religion.

How do all these people become involved in such a messed-up religion? By swallowing one lie after another. There are so many cults and false religions out there today, and not a one of them will get anyone into heaven. Which is exactly why these people will be stuck here on Earth to swallow more lies after the One True Church is raptured.

Jesus plainly said in John 14:6: *I am the way, the truth, and the life. No one can come to the Father except through me.* There is no other way to heaven except through faith in Jesus Christ. There are two simple choices: (1) No Jesus, no heaven; or (2) Know Jesus, know heaven. Which one have you chosen?

Day 112

A quick recap: Speaking of the woman, or prostitute, who represents the false religion of the Tribulation period on Earth, John is told that *[t]he scarlet beast and his ten horns ... will strip her naked, eat her flesh, and burn her remains with fire* (Revelation 17:16).

Once the Antichrist has achieved his goal of bringing the world together under one religion and one governmental power, he won't need that religion anymore, so he'll show his true colors and do away with it, demanding that he himself be worshiped.

And what about the *ten horns* or kings? *They will agree to give their authority to the scarlet beast* (Revelation 17:17a), the Antichrist. Why would they do that? *For God has put a plan into their minds, a plan that will carry out his purposes. They will agree to give their authority to the scarlet beast, and so the words of God will be fulfilled* (Revelation 17:17).

Evil destroying evil? You betcha. In Ezekiel 30:10, we read, *For this is what the Sovereign Lord says: 'By the power of King Nebuchadnezzar of Babylon, I will destroy the hordes of Egypt.'* The Lord can and will turn evil against evil.

Just as he used the evil King Nebuchadnezzar of Babylon to punish the nation of Egypt, God will use the governmental powers of the Antichrist to destroy the worldwide religion of the Tribulation, leaving the Antichrist to be followed without question, both as a political figure and as the one false god. Remember, the rest of the world leaders will have already handed over all their authority to him.

And this woman you saw in your vision represents the great city that rules over the kings of the world (Revelation 17:18). As we saw several days ago, this woman is also referred to as "Babylon," which is synonymous with evil. She is representative of the false religion itself and of this worldwide cult's headquarters city.

We're told in Revelation 16:19a that *[t]he great city of Babylon split into three sections.* Rome, in John's day, was definitely equivalent to Babylon, since it was the center of emperor worship and world power. But is Rome the seat of the ungodly religion of the Tribulation? Many people speculate, but no one knows.

As I said before, Protestants want to point at the Roman Catholic Church as being the apostate religion of the Tribulation. I don't recommend buying into that line of thought. I know many sincere believers in both Protestant and Catholic churches. There are also a lot of people in churches of every denomination who are names on church rolls and nothing more. These people will be left behind when the Rapture occurs, and they'll either repent, turn to Jesus, and be martyred for their faith, or they'll join with the others who'll become a part of the new worldwide religion. And that religion will be a mishmash of everything imaginable, plus many things beyond our imaginations.

Once the True Church is taken out of this world, there are only two options for those left behind: repent and die for your faith, or join the worldwide religion and worship the Antichrist. The far better move is to choose Jesus now and avoid the Tribulation.

Revelation 18

Day 113

Today we start Chapter 18. Let's take a look at the first three verses: *After all this I saw another angel come down from heaven with great authority, and the earth grew bright with his splendor. He gave a mighty shout: 'Babylon is fallen—that great city is fallen! She has become a home for demons. She is a hideout for every foul spirit, a hideout for every foul vulture and every foul and dreadful animal. For all the nations have fallen because of the wine of her passionate immorality. The kings of the world have committed adultery with her. Because of her desires for extravagant luxury, the merchants of the world have grown rich'* (Revelation 18:1-3).

We're still looking at Babylon, both as the woman representing the false worldwide religion of the Tribulation and as the headquarters city of that religion. *[T]hat great city is fallen!* This once-great city has become a wasteland. Why? This literal or figurative city has misled the world: *For all the nations have fallen because of the wine of her passionate immorality. The kings of the world have committed adultery with her.*

And the entire world is already in chaos. Look back through the previous chapters at the plagues that have been poured out. Still, the focus of the people isn't on repentance—it's on *extravagant luxury.*

Don't think that's merely the mindset of the Tribulation world. We need to understand that the things we see happening now are part of the ***birth pains*** Jesus talked about in Matthew 24. Yes, there'll need to be an explanation for the disappearance of those who are taken out of this world when the One True Church is removed, but the people left behind will be ready to swallow whatever rationalization they're fed.

Like the grief and horror of the attacks on 9/11, the initial shock may be great, but it won't take long for things to go back to some version of normal. I recall how packed churches became right after 9/11. It didn't take long for some folks to get over that and go on about their business—they figured they could always call on God again if there was another crisis.

But meanwhile, just as today, the majority of the world plugs along thinking only of themselves, seeking after ***extravagant luxury***. You may be thinking, *I'm not extravagant. I live in a modest home and drive a modest car.* Yet there are people all over the world who have no home, let alone a car.

Are you giving to and working with your church's missions and outreach programs to help others? Are you giving or volunteering with other organizations to help the less fortunate? In Luke 12:21, Jesus concludes the Parable of the Rich Fool, saying: ***Yes, a person is a fool to store up earthly wealth but not have a rich relationship with God.***

I read a great quote just before I began writing today's study. I wish I knew whom to credit, but I believe it's the perfect closing statement for all of us to think on: "How can you say you want to spend eternity with Jesus if you don't spend time with him now?" That sure stepped on my toes. How about yours?

Day 114

Yesterday we saw Babylon both as the woman representing the false worldwide religion of the Tribulation and as the headquarters city of that religion. The voice of *another angel ... with great authority ... gave a mighty shout, 'Babylon is fallen—that great city is fallen!'* (from Revelation 18:1-2a).

Then I heard another voice calling from heaven, 'Come away from her, my people. Do not take part in her sins, or you will be punished with her. For her sins are piled as high as heaven, and God remembers her evil deeds. Do to her as she has done to others. Double her penalty for all her evil deeds. She brewed a cup of terror for others, so brew twice as much for her. She glorified herself and lived in luxury, so match it now with torment and sorrow. She boasted in her heart, 'I am queen on my throne. I am no helpless widow, and I have no reason to mourn.' Therefore, these plagues will overtake her in a single day—death and mourning and famine. She will be completely consumed by fire, for the Lord God who judges her is mighty (Revelation 18:4-8).

Remember, the timeframe in the Revelation isn't necessarily chronological. Here we learn more about the destruction of the city referred to as Babylon, not only the worldwide religion's headquarters, but also an important commercial center.

The second voice we hear in Chapter 18 calls out: *Come away from her, my people. Do not take part in her sins, or you will be punished with her.* How can God's people be in this sinful place during the Tribulation? One of two ways: (1) This is before the

229

Mark of the Beast is imposed on everyone; or (2) the Mark has been imposed, but not all the people who have turned to Jesus after the Tribulation have been caught and killed by the Antichrist's forces. They could be in hiding within this very place.

This *voice calling from heaven* first addresses the remaining believers on Earth and then the forces God will use to punish Babylon, the *woman sitting on a scarlet beast that had seven heads and ten horns* (Revelation 17:3b): *Do to her as she has done to others. Double her penalty for all her evil deeds. She brewed a cup of terror for others, so brew twice as much for her. She glorified herself and lived in luxury, so match it now with torment and sorrow.*

Who's going to destroy this Babylon? We saw the answer in Revelation 17: *The ten horns of the beast are ten kings .... The scarlet beast and his ten horns all hate the prostitute. They will strip her naked, eat her flesh, and burn her remains with fire. For God has put a plan into their minds, a plan that will carry out his purposes. They will agree to give their authority to the scarlet beast, and so the words of God will be fulfilled. And this woman you saw in your vision represents the great city that rules over the kings of the world* (Revelation 17:12a, 16-18).

Let me remind us: Just as he used the evil King Nebuchadnezzar of Babylon to punish the nation of Egypt, God will use the governmental powers of the Antichrist to destroy the worldwide religion of the Tribulation, leaving the Antichrist to be followed without question, both as a political figure and as the one false god. Meanwhile, Babylon is completely confident in her position of wealth and authority. She has no idea she's about to meet her final destruction.

A lot of people living today are in the same boat. They're healthy, wealthy, and think themselves wise. They feel untouchable and unsinkable. But no one is. Every human is accountable to God and one day *each of us will give a personal account to God* (Romans 14:12). Have you given any thought to what you'll say?

Day 115

Yesterday we saw Babylon as: (1) the false religion itself; (2) the headquarters of that worldwide religion; and (3) the economic hub of the self-centered, money-obsessed city of *extravagant luxury* (Revelation 18:3) within the Tribulation world.

I reminded us once more that the timeframe in the Revelation isn't necessarily chronological. That said, at whatever point the Antichrist turns against this so-called Babylon, represented by the *woman sitting on a scarlet beast* (Revelation 17:3b), that Beast, the Antichrist, will destroy her and demand that he alone be worshiped. All according to God's plan, even though they foolishly won't realize this.

And what is the people's reaction? Revelation 18:9-19 (BSB) gives a good description. I'm only going to post an excerpt here, but I urge you to go back and read the passage in its entirety.

Then the kings of the earth who committed sexual immorality and lived in luxury with her will weep and wail at the sight of the smoke rising from the fire that consumes her. In fear of her torment, they will stand at a distance and cry out.... And the merchants of the earth will weep and mourn over her, because there is no one left to buy their cargo.... The merchants who sold these things and grew their wealth from her will stand at a distance, in fear of her torment. They will weep and mourn.... Every shipmaster, passenger, and sailor, and all who make their living from the sea, will stand at a distance and cry out at the sight of the smoke rising from the fire that consumes her. 'What city was ever like this great city?' they will exclaim. Then they will throw dust on their heads as they weep and mourn and cry out.

But while those who belong to the world are heartbroken at the great city's demise, those who belong to the King of Kings and Lord of Lords are celebrating: ***Rejoice over her, O heaven, O saints and apostles and prophets, because for you God has pronounced his judgment against her*** (Revelation 18:20).

God has done to this city, the center of worship and economic power for the ***woman sitting on a scarlet beast*** (Revelation 17:3b) who was ***drunk with the blood of God's holy people*** (Revelation 17:6a), what she desired to do to God's people. And while the martyred believers celebrate in heaven, the kings, who have surrendered their power to the Antichrist, and all the others who had adored this Babylon, will look on in horror.

The Tribulation period will be seven years—such a short time in the span of creation. But that time will be indescribably difficult for those who have waited until after the Rapture of the Church to turn to Jesus. For those who continue to reject him and put their allegiance with the Antichrist, unimaginable terror awaits not only on Earth, but into eternity.

We'll dig deeper into this passage tomorrow.

Day 116

We've begun our look at Revelation 18:9-19 concerning the people's reaction to the destruction of the city called Babylon. Now let's examine what the different people actually have to say about its destruction. I urge you to read the entire passage, since I'm only including specific portions.

And the kings of the world who committed adultery with her and enjoyed her great luxury ... cry out, ... 'In a single moment God's judgment came on you' (from Verses 9-10).

The merchants of the world will weep and mourn for her.... 'The fancy things you loved so much are gone,' they cry. 'All your luxuries and splendor are gone forever, never to be yours again' (from Verses 11-14).

The merchants who became wealthy by selling her these things will ... cry out, ... 'In a single moment all the wealth of the city is gone!' (from Verses 15-17a).

And all the captains of the merchant ships and their passengers and sailors and crews will ... cry out ... 'The shipowners became wealthy by transporting her great wealth on the seas. In a single moment it is all gone' (from Verses 17b-19).

One moment everything was business as usual, and the next moment everything was destroyed. We need to remember that all this earthly stuff is just that: momentary. We need to obey what Jesus told us to do: *Don't store up treasures here on earth.... Store your treasures in heaven* (Matthew 6:19a, 20a).

How did this sudden destruction come about? We see repeated images of fire and smoke, but this could be figuratively or literally the fiery judgment of God. What we are shown is the finality of Babylon's fate: ***Then a mighty angel picked up a boulder the size of a huge millstone. He threw it into the ocean and shouted, 'Just like this, the great city Babylon will be thrown down with violence and will never be found again'*** (Revelation 18:21).

To put this angel's actions into modern-day vernacular, he shows John that Babylon's destruction will be like throwing that boulder into the ocean—it's going to sink like a rock, ***never*** [to] ***be found again***.

But before we move from this passage, let's take a further look at ***her great wealth***. What was being brought out of and into Babylon? We'll find out tomorrow.

Day 117

How did the city called Babylon acquire her **great wealth**? (Revelation 18:19). *She bought great quantities of gold, silver, jewels, and pearls; fine linen, purple, silk, and scarlet cloth; things made of fragrant thyine wood, ivory goods, and objects made of expensive wood; and bronze, iron, and marble. She also bought cinnamon, spice, incense, myrrh, frankincense, wine, olive oil, fine flour, wheat, cattle, sheep, horses, wagons, and bodies—that is, human slaves* (Revelation 18:12-13).

No doubt what Babylon brought in was sold and traded on the world market. Basically, we see eight types of purchases, all bought in **great quantities**:

(1) Jewelry: **gold, silver, jewels, and pearls**; (2) The very finest fabric for clothing and home decorating: **fine linen, purple, silk, and scarlet cloth**; (3) Top-of-the-line furniture and decorative pieces: **things made of fragrant thyine wood, ivory goods, and objects made of expensive wood; and bronze, iron, and marble**; (4) Spices for seasoning, as well as home and body fragrance: **cinnamon, spice, incense, myrrh, frankincense**; (5) Luxury items for cooking and entertaining: **wine, olive oil, fine flour, wheat**; (6) Livestock: **cattle, sheep**; (7) The latest in transportation: **horses, wagons**; (8) And humans: **bodies—that is, human slaves**.

Most of this list is pretty self-explanatory, but when it comes to the transportation—**horses, wagons**—I think it'd be fair to compare the horses and wagons—also translated as **chariots**—with Corvettes and Porsches today. None of these things were necessities. They were the extravagant luxuries of Earth's self-centered, worldly-minded population.

Human trafficking is also included. With the immorality and perversion that will be interwoven with this sick worldwide religion, represented by Babylon and headquartered in a city referred to by that name, men and women will be bought and sold for unthinkable purposes. And, yes, human trafficking happens today on a much larger scale than we want to even think about, but in the Tribulation world, it won't be a hidden evil—it'll be openly flaunted. Sex shops and pornography will be commonplace, and only an inkling of what will be available in the sex trade.

No one will be safe. No one.

Day 118

We've already been introduced to the angel who threw the boulder into the ocean, showing John that Babylon's destruction will be like that boulder hitting the water—it's going to sink like a rock. That same passage goes on to say that the angel *shouted* (Revelation 18:21a) as he threw in the boulder. What did the angel say?

Just like this, the great city Babylon will be thrown down with violence and will never be found again. The sound of harps, singers, flutes, and trumpets will never be heard in you again. No craftsmen and no trades will ever be found in you again. The sound of the mill will never be heard in you again. The light of a lamp will never shine in you again. The happy voices of brides and grooms will never be heard in you again. For your merchants were the greatest in the world, and you deceived the nations with your sorceries. In your streets flowed the blood of the prophets and of God's holy people and the blood of people slaughtered all over the world (Revelation 18:21b-24).

Babylon, the false worldwide religion and its city headquarters, will be utterly and permanently destroyed. No parties or happy celebrations with *harps, singers, flutes, and trumpets*. While all heaven is rejoicing—see the music and singing in Revelation 15 as just one example—Babylon's partying days are over. And there's no more business-as-usual: *No craftsmen and no trades.* No workforce, no *sound of the mill*.

The light of a lamp will never shine in you again. The false light of the Tribulation's worldwide religion will be snuffed out. This passage reminds me of Jesus' words in Matthew 8:12, 22:13

237

and 25:30 where he speaks of lost people being cast into outer darkness, *where there will be weeping and gnashing of teeth*. It'd be well worth your time to read all those passages and their connected verses.

The happy voices of brides and grooms will never be heard in you again. Couples getting married are looking to their future together. For the people of Babylon, there is no earthly future.

For your merchants were the greatest in the world, and you deceived the nations with your sorceries. Don't miss this: the word translated *sorceries* is the very same Greek word *pharmakeia* from which we get our word "pharmacy." The abuse of prescription and street drugs is already rampant today, and the use of drugs will undoubtedly be an integral part of the worldwide false religion as the entire Tribulation world is lured into a hell-bound stupor.

Before this, though, anyone who had opposed the followers of this unholy religion was eliminated with no more concern than if they were swatting flies: *In your streets flowed the blood of the prophets and of God's holy people and the blood of people slaughtered all over the world.* The word translated *slaughtered* here specifically refers to those who have been violently murdered.

Babylon, the false worldwide religion of the Tribulation period, will seek out and murder every person who doesn't follow their teaching. And the only ones who'll oppose it are those who have committed their hearts and lives to Jesus Christ after the Rapture of the Church. Yes, those believers will die horrible deaths, but they'll be raised to eternal life with no memory of the terrors they endured. Not so for those who join with the Antichrist. Their suffering will be forever. We need to warn others about that.

Revelation 19

Day 119

As we leave Revelation 18 and move into Chapter 19, we go from the horrors of the destruction on Earth to the joyous celebration in heaven: *After this I heard a sound like the roar of a great multitude in heaven, shouting: 'Hallelujah! Salvation and glory and power belong to our God! For His judgments are true and just. He has judged the great prostitute who corrupted the earth with her immorality. He has avenged the blood of his servants that was poured out by her hand.' And a second time they called out: 'Hallelujah! Her smoke ascends forever and ever.' And the twenty-four elders and the four living creatures fell down and worshiped God who sits on the throne, saying: 'Amen, Hallelujah!'*

Then a voice came from the throne, saying: 'Praise our God, all you who serve him, and those who fear him, small and great alike!' (Revelation 19:1-5).

Who's doing all this celebrating in heaven? First, we see *a great multitude*. These are the ones saved during the Tribulation. As the angel in Revelation 18 shouted concerning the destruction of Babylon: *In your streets flowed the blood of the prophets and of God's holy people and the blood of people slaughtered all over the world* (Revelation 18:24). Those who have accepted Jesus Christ as Lord and Savior during the Tribulation have been martyred, and the time for Babylon's destruction has arrived. The only exceptions are the 144,000 Jewish special witnesses we saw earlier. (See Revelation 7:3-8 and Revelation 9:4.)

Celebrating with the *great multitude* are *the twenty-four elders and the four living creatures*. Note that both of the shouts of the *great multitude* are recorded by John as beginning with the word *Hallelujah!* And *the twenty-four elders and the four living creatures* cry out to the Lord: *Amen, Hallelujah!*

This is no mumbled praise. This is no casual worship service. This is all-out ecstasy. The word *Hallelujah!* requires an exclamation point because it's literally an imperative command to "Praise the Lord!" And heaven is doing just that.

But in addition to the *great multitude* and *the twenty-four elders and the four living creatures,* we hear another voice: *Then a voice came from the throne, saying: 'Praise our God, all you who serve him, and those who fear him, small and great alike!'* (Revelation 19:5). We aren't told who this is, but it's most likely one of the cherubim at God's throne and he is unmistakably excited!

We know what's coming. We know who's going to keep those who belong to him from that terrible time. And we should be thanking him right now. Remember his words to the church of Philadelphia*? Because you have obeyed my command to persevere, I will protect you from the great time of testing that will come upon the whole world to test those who belong to this world* (Revelation 3:10).

And who is the Church? You are. I am. Every person who has committed their heart and life to Jesus. And Church, Jesus is speaking to all His people. Have you obeyed Christ's *command to persevere*? If you have, then you can claim his promise: *I will protect you from the great time of testing.* And having learned a lot more about what's going to happen, we have all the more reason to tell the Lord how grateful we are.

Day 120

Today we move from the heavenly celebration of the destruction of Babylon to the celebration of the climactic event, the extravaganza of extravaganzas, in heaven: *And I heard a sound like the roar of a great multitude, like the rushing of many waters, and like a mighty rumbling of thunder, crying out: 'Hallelujah! For our Lord God, the Almighty, reigns. Let us rejoice and be glad and give him the glory. For the marriage of the Lamb has come, and his bride has made herself ready. She was given clothing of fine linen, bright and pure.' For the fine linen she wears is the righteous acts of the saints* (Revelation 19:6-8, BSB).

[A] great multitude is *crying out* and their first word is the same one we saw yesterday: *Hallelujah!* a command that all heaven "Praise the Lord!" The moment they've all been waiting for has come: *[T]he marriage of the Lamb ... and his bride has made herself ready.*

For our Lord God, the Almighty, reigns. Let us rejoice and be glad and give him the glory. The word translated *reigns* means to rule over with complete control. God is never out of control, even when things seem to be in total chaos. Yes, he is allowing Satan a time of power in this world; however, now and even in the Tribulation period, his power will be limited. But when Jesus Christ returns to Earth, the Lord will be in absolute control over everything.

This is an important spot to remind you of what we looked at early on in this study: Don't confuse Jesus' Second Coming with the Rapture. In the Rapture, the Church is taken up into glory;

Jesus doesn't set foot on the Earth. He calls his own to join him in heaven. In the Second Coming, Jesus returns to Earth, along with all his people, to end the reign of *the prince of this world* (John 12:31, NIV) after the seven years of the Tribulation.

If you look back at the narrative of Jesus' birth, you'll see Matthew's condensed version of how the birth of Jesus Christ came about: *His mother Mary was pledged in marriage to Joseph, but before they came together, she was found to be with Child through the Holy Spirit. Because Joseph her husband was a righteous man and was unwilling to disgrace her publicly, he resolved to divorce her quietly* (Matthew 1:18-19, BSB).

While some translations say "break the engagement," this and other translations more appropriately say *divorce*. Engagement was a binding contract. For all intents and purposes, the couple was married, even though the marriage had yet to be consummated. Meanwhile, the bride was to spend that betrothal period getting ready to be the wife of her groom, and the groom was to spend that betrothal period preparing a home for himself and his bride.

The moment you accepted Jesus Christ as your Lord and Savior, you became a part of his Bride, the One True Church. From that moment forward, your job was to prepare yourself in every way to be the kind of bride your Bridegroom deserves: *[P]ure and holy* (1 Corinthians 1:30b).

As Jesus told his disciples, *I am going to prepare a place for you. I would not tell you this if it were not so. And after I go and prepare a place for you, I will come back and take you to myself, so that you will be where I am* (John 14:2b-3, GNT).

I guarantee the Bridegroom is doing his part to be ready for the Marriage. How about you, Bride? Are you making preparation for the Big Day?

Day 121

We left off at the announcement that ***the marriage of the Lamb has come, and his bride has made herself ready*** (Revelation 19:7, BSB). Today we begin with Revelation 19:9: ***And the angel said to me, 'Write this: Blessed are those who are invited to the wedding feast of the Lamb.' And he added, "These are true words that come from God.'***

Blessed are those who are invited to the wedding feast of the Lamb. There is no greater blessing than to be part of the glorious Bride of Christ. The great British evangelist Charles Haddon Spurgeon compared the Church to Cinderella, ignored and mistreated by so many—just like Jesus. Yet when Jesus returns to judge the Earth, we'll be with him and recognized for who we are: the spotless Bride of Christ.

Then I fell down at his feet to worship him, but he said, 'No, don't worship me. I am a servant of God, just like you and your brothers and sisters who testify about their faith in Jesus (Revelation 19:10a).

Then I fell down at his feet to worship him. Overcome with excitement at what was happening, John, for the second time, falls at the feet of a heavenly angel who immediately rebukes him and reminds him: ***I am a servant of God, just like you and your brothers and sisters who testify about their faith in Jesus.***

In the Judy-an translation, the angel said to John, "I'm just like you, merely a servant of God." But he didn't stop there, did he? He said, ***like you and your brothers and sisters***. But he didn't stop there, either. He identified exactly who were the real, honest-

243

to-goodness, heaven-bound believers who make up the One True Church: *[T]hose who testify about their faith in Jesus.*

May I be bold here and say, if you don't talk about your faith, you have no faith. And if you don't live out your faith, you have no faith. What was it James said? *[B]lessing and cursing come pouring out of the same mouth. Surely, my brothers and sisters, this is not right! Does a spring of water bubble out with both fresh water and bitter water? Does a fig tree produce olives, or a grapevine produce figs? No, and you can't draw fresh water from a salty spring* (James 3:10-12).

All of us make mistakes, but if a professing believer can praise the Lord one minute and pitch a fit the next, they're a terrible witness. They're showing the world that it's okay to live both ways. I side with James on this and say: *[My] brothers and sisters, this is not right!*

If a person can flip-flop like that on a regular basis, I believe it's time for that person to back up and reexamine their commitment to Christ. When a person truly commits their life to Jesus Christ, the Holy Spirit comes to indwell that person and they become a newborn babe in the Kingdom of God. And healthy babies grow. And mature. I can tell you from personal experience that if a growing Christian chooses to do, say, or think contrary to what is pleasing to God, the Holy Spirit will convict them.

And if that person continues in wrongful actions, words, or thoughts, the Heavenly Father will get their attention, if not flat-out take them to the woodshed. And believe me, nobody wants to be on the receiving end of that lesson.

Are you a consistent Christian? Do the people you hang around with all week see the same person your church sees on Sunday? Matter of fact, does your church even see you on Sundays? I urge you, as a member of the Bride of Christ: be as faithful to your Bridegroom as he's been to you.

Day 122

In his excitement over the angel's announcement about the Marriage of the Lamb, John falls at the angel's feet and is promptly told: *I am a servant of God, just like you and your brothers and sisters who testify about their faith in Jesus. Worship only God* (from Revelation 19:10).

Worship only God. This simple three-word sentence is critical to living in obedience to God. We don't worship angels. We don't worship creation. We don't worship anything manmade. And we certainly don't worship other people. Our spouses, parents, siblings, children, grandchildren, and friends may be precious to us, but our love and commitment to any of them should never come before our love and commitment to Jesus Christ. If he's not first in your life, he's not God in your life.

Then the angel closes his statement with these words: *For the essence of prophecy is to give a clear witness for Jesus* (Revelation 19:10b). Or as the BSB words it, *For the testimony of Jesus is the spirit of prophecy!*

Meaning what? Every word of prophecy from Genesis to Revelation is pointing us to Jesus. And the purpose of prophecy is stated here: *[T]o give a clear witness for Jesus.* It's not about predicting the future—Jesus already said, *[N]o one knows the day or hour when these things will happen, not even the angels in heaven or the Son himself. Only the Father knows* (Mark 13:32).

I can't begin to claim a deep understanding of the Triune God, the Holy Trinity—God the Father, Jesus the Son, and the Holy Spirit. I have to go with what Jesus said in Mark 10:15: we're to *receive the Kingdom of God like a child*. Maybe someone much wiser and better educated than me can fully understand this stuff, but, for me, there's a lot I must simply accept with the faith of *a child*. If my Father says it's so, then it is. And that settles it.

There's no way I can begin to figure out how God the Father withholds from Jesus the Son the information concerning *the day or hour when these things will happen*. But what I do know is this: at some moment in time—and I believe that moment is in the near future—the Father will say to the Son just what that wonderful song of praise, "Midnight Cry," says he will: "Son, go get my children." And when God the Father speaks those words, the Son will call his own out of this Earth and into their eternal home in glory.

Day 123

The wedding feast of the Lamb has been announced and the angel making the announcement explains: ***For the essence of prophecy is to give a clear witness for Jesus*** (Revelation 19:10b). Those who are truly born again, those who will be part of the Bride of Christ, are those who **give a clear witness for Jesus**. Being a true believer is more than mouthed words or being baptized. It's sincere repentance, producing an inward change— heart, mind and spirit—that also shows on the outside. True faith changes our walk, our talk, and our thoughts. For those who have made that change, receiving Jesus Christ as Lord and Savior, the warnings of Revelation hold no terror, but only joy for what's to come.

Then I saw heaven opened, and a white horse was standing there. Its rider was named Faithful and True, for he judges fairly and wages a righteous war. His eyes were like flames of fire, and on his head were many crowns. A name was written on him that no one understood except himself. He wore a robe dipped in blood, and his title was the Word of God. The armies of heaven, dressed in the finest of pure white linen, followed him on white horses. From his mouth came a sharp sword to strike down the nations. He will rule them with an iron rod. He will release the fierce wrath of God, the Almighty, like juice flowing from a winepress. On his robe at his thigh was written this title: King of all kings and Lord of all lords (Revelation 19:11-16).

Then I saw heaven opened, and a white horse was standing there. Everything has been building to this moment when the Lamb returns as the Lion. Only the elite of the military had the privilege of riding a horse. Jesus not only has a horse, but *a white horse*, the color of victory and the color of the *white robes* (ISV) we see on the faithful elders in Revelation 4:4.

Its rider was named Faithful and True, for he judges fairly and wages a righteous war. Jesus Christ, the *Faithful and True*, isn't out to seek power; all power is already in his hands. The time has come for him to set wrong things right, so he will wage *a righteous war* against those who have rejected him and harmed those who are his children.

Jesus loves his family, and any harm that comes to them here will one day be avenged. And that doesn't just go for those left behind during the Tribulation. That goes for every person in every age who in any way mistreats or misleads one of God's children: *But if you cause one of these little ones who trusts in me to fall into sin, it would be better for you to be thrown into the sea with a large millstone hung around your neck* (Mark 9:42).

We've only made it through the first verse in this passage. If you know Jesus, this is exciting reading. Stay with me.

Day 124

Let's re-read Revelation 19:11-16 and then we'll take a deeper look into John's description of Jesus as the Righteous Judge: *Then I saw heaven opened, and a white horse was standing there. Its rider was named Faithful and True, for he judges fairly and wages a righteous war. His eyes were like flames of fire, and on his head were many crowns. A name was written on him that no one understood except himself. He wore a robe dipped in blood, and his title was the Word of God. The armies of heaven, dressed in the finest of pure white linen, followed him on white horses. From his mouth came a sharp sword to strike down the nations. He will rule them with an iron rod. He will release the fierce wrath of God, the Almighty, like juice flowing from a winepress. On his robe at his thigh was written this title: King of all kings and Lord of all lords* (Revelation 19:11-16).

We covered Verse 11 yesterday. Verses 12 and 13 give us John's description of Jesus: *His eyes were like flames of fire, and on his head were many crowns. A name was written on him that no one understood except himself. He wore a robe dipped in blood, and his title was the Word of God.* Jesus' eyes as *flames of fire* indicate his all-penetrating gaze. Nothing is hidden from him.

The identity of his *many crowns* is a matter of debate for a lot of Bible scholars. First, though, let me clarify that these crowns are not the *stephanos*, the crowns like laurel wreaths given to competition winners. These crowns are *diadema*, crowns only a royal ruler would wear.

In olden days, a conquering king would take the crowns of the kings he conquered, so some believe these crowns are the ones taken from the earthly rulers during the Tribulation. I don't agree. The King of Kings and Lord of Lords needs no earthly crown. Like *the cattle on a thousand hills* (Psalm 50:10b), he already owns everything. He has authority over everything. And now the time has come for him to use that authority in judgment against those who have rejected him. His crowns are his own, showing total authority over all things in all creation.

A name was written on him that no one understood except himself. Here's another spot where Bible scholars speculate their little hearts out, but the point is he didn't tell John what the name was, and he isn't telling us.

However, if we flip back again to his letter to the church in Philadelphia, we read: *All who are victorious will become pillars in the Temple of my God, and they will never have to leave it. And I will write on them the name of my God, and they will be citizens in the city of my God—the New Jerusalem that comes down from heaven from my God. And I will also write on them my new name* (Revelation 3:12).

The day I accepted Jesus Christ as my Lord and Savior, I was adopted into the family of God. And that means I bear my Father's name. And so do you, and all who've put their faith in Jesus. We have so much to look forward to! How did Paul say it? *We ... wait with eager hope for the day when God will give us our full rights as his adopted children* (Romans 8:23b).

If Jesus is your Savior, He's also your Abba Father. Your Daddy. And one day, I believe he'll reveal to us that special family name. No more Smiths, Joneses, Bateses, or anything else. We'll all have one name, our Father's name, and we'll all live together in perfect harmony. Won't that be wonderful!

We made it through Verse 12 today. We'll pick up on Verse 13 tomorrow.

Day 125

His eyes were like flames of fire, and on His head were many crowns. A name was written on Him that no one understood except himself. He wore a robe dipped in blood, and his title was the Word of God (Revelation 19:12-13).

Why is Jesus' robe **dipped in blood**? There are sure some ideas about that! Some say it's his own blood. Some say it's the blood of his enemies. Let's look at one possibility at a time. First, why would Jesus be covered in his own blood? Christ's blood was shed for the redemption of our sins. He is the Once-And-For-All Perfect Sacrifice. At this point, every person who has ever lived on Planet Earth and has put their faith in him has already been washed in his blood. That work is finished. Those he will now confront have no opportunity to repent.

So is it the blood of Jesus' enemies on his robe? Considering he's coming to render judgment and deal with all of those who will choose to fight against him, why would he show up already covered in their blood?

Let me throw out a third possibility: what if his robe is covered in the blood of the martyrs, those who held to their faith even as the Beast and his cohorts tortured and killed them? I believe this is certainly a possibility, and I believe that someway, somehow, those enemies of God will know exactly whose blood they're seeing. And it will serve as a crimson reminder of their persecution of God's children. These enemies of the cross will answer to those martyred children's Father.

The one they see coming bears the title of *the Word of God*. Years before he was given the Revelation of Jesus Christ, John wrote: *In the beginning the Word already existed. The Word was with God, and the Word was God. He existed in the beginning with God. God created everything through him, and nothing was created except through him. The Word gave life to everything that was created, and his life brought light to everyone* (John 1:1-4).

Jesus Christ is God. He is the Living Word. There has never been any point at which he didn't already exist. When a person rebels against Jesus, they're rebelling against their Creator. They're rebelling against the One who gave them life and offers them eternal life. And as John tells us: *His life brought light to everyone.*

But not everyone believes in the Light. Those who reject him choose instead *deeds of evil and darkness* (Ephesians 5:11). But not to worry. As John declares: *The light shines in the darkness, and the darkness can never extinguish it* (John 1:5). Jesus Christ is the Victor, and tomorrow we'll see the army who's coming back to Earth with him.

Day 126

As John saw Jesus ride out of the heavens on his white horse, he described him: *His eyes were like flames of fire, and on his head were many crowns. A name was written on him that no one understood except himself. He wore a robe dipped in blood, and his title was the Word of God* (Revelation 19:12-13).

What else did John see? *The armies of heaven, dressed in the finest of pure white linen, followed him on white horses* (Revelation 19:14). Just a few verses earlier, John described the Bride prepared for her Marriage to the Lamb: *She has been given the finest of pure white linen to wear* (Revelation 19:8a). That's us, folks. As Revelation 17:14 has already told us: *[H]is called and chosen and faithful ones will be with him.*

But note: the word *armies* is plural. Not only do the saints of God ride with the Lord, there's also an army of heavenly angels coming with us. In Matthew 16, we read where Jesus told his disciples about his impending death and *Peter took him aside and began to reprimand him for saying such things* (Matthew 16:22a). I can't even imagine!

After Jesus dealt with Peter, he told all his disciples: *For the Son of Man will come with his angels in the glory of his Father* (Matthew 16:27a). In the Revelation, we see an army of saints and an army of angels—talk about mighty forces!—and all under the command of the Righteous Judge and Lion of Judah.

From His mouth came a sharp sword to strike down the nations. He will rule them with an iron rod. He will release the fierce wrath of God, the Almighty, like juice flowing from a winepress (Revelation 19:15).

Is Jesus coming with a sword literally coming out of his mouth? Of course not. This sword is the Word, which he will use *to strike down the nations*. And the word there for *strike* means to slay. Every person remaining on Planet Earth has had multiple opportunities to believe the Word of God. Yet they have rejected it and they have rejected the one it represents. The Living Word, Jesus Christ, the Righteous Judge, will render judgment.

He will rule them with an iron rod. He will release the fierce wrath of God, the Almighty, like juice flowing from a winepress. Don't misunderstand the first part of this passage. The word *rod* can also be translated as "staff" or "scepter." Jesus will return to rule over all, but his first act is to slay all those who have rejected him. He's not going to force conversion on the unsaved. He's going to wipe them off the Earth with *the fierce wrath of God, the Almighty*.

On his robe at his thigh was written this title: King of all kings and Lord of all lords (Revelation 19:16). I won't go into great depth on all this, but some Bible scholars believe Jesus has not just a name written on him—the name *no one understood except himself* —but many other names as well. After all, He's the Lamb of God, the Lion of Judah, the Righteous Judge, and he holds title to so many other wonderful names: Emmanuel, the Bread of Life, the Alpha and Omega, our Bridegroom, Faithful and True, Son of God, our Great High Priest, the Door, the Way, the Truth, the Light of the World, and dozens more titles of honor.

May I suggest he wears a crown for every title he holds: *[O]n his head were many crowns.* And visible to all as he comes in victory is this name: *King of all kings and Lord of all lords.* He's the Everything. Don't you love him!

Day 127

Then I saw an angel standing in the sun, shouting to the vultures flying high in the sky: 'Come! Gather together for the great banquet God has prepared. Come and eat the flesh of kings, generals, and strong warriors; of horses and their riders; and of all humanity, both free and slave, small and great.'

Then I saw the beast and the kings of the world and their armies gathered together to fight against the one sitting on the horse and his army. And the beast was captured, and with him the false prophet who did mighty miracles on behalf of the beast—miracles that deceived all who had accepted the mark of the beast and who worshiped his statue. Both the beast and his false prophet were thrown alive into the fiery lake of burning sulfur. Their entire army was killed by the sharp sword that came from the mouth of the one riding the white horse. And the vultures all gorged themselves on the dead bodies (Revelation 19:17-21).

Chapter 19 ends with what we call the Battle of Armageddon. Note the angel's call: *Gather together for the great banquet God has prepared.* Those who passed up their opportunity to attend the Wedding Feast of the Lamb aren't invited to lunch here—they'll *be* lunch, as the scavengers *eat the flesh of kings, generals, and strong warriors; of horses and their riders; and of all humanity, both free and slave, small and great.*

Lost humanity—*all who had accepted the mark of the beast and who worshiped his statue*—will die: *Their entire army was killed by the sharp sword that came from the mouth of the one riding the white horse.* But that's only their physical deaths. Revelation 20:15 says: *And anyone whose name was not found recorded in the Book of Life was thrown into the lake of fire.* But not before standing in front of Jesus at the Great White Throne of Judgment.

Both the beast and his false prophet, however, are *thrown alive into the fiery lake of burning sulfur.* These two are the only people in the Bible to be cast alive into hell. This is the fire that will take their physical lives but leave their spirits to suffer forever.

Hell is real, and God sends no one there. So how does anyone end up there? By choosing it. Choose Jesus and choose life. Reject him and you've chosen damnation. Not knowing Jesus as your Lord and Savior isn't the trivial matter some people think. It's a life or death decision.

Revelation 20

Day 128

Then I saw an angel coming down from heaven with the key to the bottomless pit and a heavy chain in his hand. He seized the dragon—that old serpent, who is the devil, Satan— and bound Him in chains for a thousand years. The angel threw Him into the bottomless pit, which he then shut and locked so Satan could not deceive the nations anymore until the thousand years were finished. Afterward he must be released for a little while (Revelation 20:1-3).

Look at the end of today's passage: *Afterward he must be released for a little while.* What! After locking Satan away for 1,000 years, God will let him out again? I'm afraid so. But only *for a little while.* How long is that? The Bible doesn't tell us. But we'll get into that a little later.

For now, though, we're at the end of the Tribulation. The Battle of Armageddon has taken place and countless numbers of the lost *who had accepted the mark of the beast and who worshiped his statue* (Revelation 19:20b)—but apparently not all mankind—have experienced physical death. The people left on Earth will have the privilege of living in a Satan-free world with Jesus reigning over all while Satan is locked in *the bottomless pit*.

Who can possibly be left on Earth after the Judgment? I see only one explanation, and that's that a small number of those who repented and accepted Jesus Christ as Lord and Savior after the Rapture survived being slaughtered by the regime of the Unholy Trinity. No unsaved person could possibly survive, since Jesus'

257

return means the final destruction of all who've rejected him.

While the Bible doesn't tell us exactly what transpires during the Millennium, it's likely that life on Earth will include people living, dying, and being born just as today. Nothing indicates that those on Earth who survive the Tribulation will live throughout the entire 1,000 years.

Then I saw thrones, and the people sitting on them had been given the authority to judge. And I saw the souls of those who had been beheaded for their testimony about Jesus and for proclaiming the word of God. They had not worshiped the beast or his statue, nor accepted his mark on their foreheads or their hands. They all came to life again, and they reigned with Christ for a thousand years.

This is the first resurrection. (The rest of the dead did not come back to life until the thousand years had ended.) Blessed and holy are those who share in the first resurrection. For them the second death holds no power, but they will be priests of God and of Christ and will reign with Him a thousand years (Revelation 20:4-6).

It's so important not to pull out one verse or passage without understanding other passages that relate to the same topic. Here, it sounds as though the martyrs of the Tribulation will be the only ones reigning with Jesus during the Millennium. But look back at what Jesus said in his letter to the church at Thyatira, which, like the other six letters, is intended for the Church of all ages: *To all who are victorious, who obey me to the very end, To them I will give authority over all the nations* (Revelation 2:26).

The entire Bride of Christ, as his army of saints, will already be with him when he returns at the end of the Tribulation (see Revelation 19:14). After the Battle of Armageddon and at the start of Christ's Millennial Reign, those who were martyred during the Tribulation will return to life and also reign *with Christ for a thousand years. This is the first resurrection.*

The rest of the dead did not come back to life until the thousand years had ended. Who are these people? I'll save that answer and more until tomorrow.

Day 129

Yesterday I reminded us how important it is not to pull out one verse or passage without understanding other passages that relate to the same topic. What we read in Revelation 20:4 made it sound as though the martyrs of the Tribulation will be the only ones reigning with Jesus during the Millennium: *I saw the souls of those who had been beheaded for their testimony about Jesus and for proclaiming the word of God.... They all came to life again, and they reigned with Christ for a thousand years* (from Revelation 20:4b).

But if we read back through what we've already studied, we know that the entire Church, the Bride of Christ, will be with Jesus during his Millennial Reign. Those who died believing in Jesus throughout all the ages and those who were raptured as the Tribulation period began will all be with him.

So what does it mean when we read: *This is the first resurrection. (The rest of the dead did not come back to life until the thousand years had ended.) Blessed and holy are those who share in the first resurrection* (Revelation 20:5-6a).

Contrary to what we may have thought, the unsaved may not be roasting away in hell right now. Then where are they? As far as what we're shown in Scripture, only the Beast (the Antichrist) and the False Prophet are in hell because we're told that, after the Battle of Armageddon, *Both the beast and his false prophet were thrown alive into the fiery lake of burning sulfur* (Revelation 19:20b).

While some Bible scholars believe hell is already full of lost people, others believe unbelievers are in a "soul sleep," awaiting the Final Judgment. About those lines of thought, I'll say this much: it's difficult to think of God plucking people out of hell just to stand at the Great White Throne of Judgment and then being sentenced back into hell. But consider what we see today: prisoners held in jail for long periods of time before their actual trial and sentencing. So it's possible and even likely that those who die without Jesus are immediately sent to hell. I hope you'll also take the time to read Luke 16:19-31.

But what about the saved? Where are they when they die? According to Jesus' own words to the repentant thief on the cross, *[T]oday you will be with Me in paradise* (Luke 23:43b). And Paul said, *[T]o be absent from the body, and to be present with the Lord* (2 Corinthians 5:8b, KJV). When a believer experiences physical death, he is translated from earthly life to eternal life. *This is the first resurrection.*

Blessed and holy are those who share in the first resurrection. For them the second death holds no power (Revelation 20:6a). What's *the second death*? Those who die without faith in Jesus Christ die physically first and spiritually second. They aren't resurrected to new life as are believers, but instead, spend eternity in a place of unending torment.

Back to the Millennial Reign of Christ. Believers will be with him. And throughout the Millennium, the surviving people of Earth will live under the rule of the Righteous King Jesus with no evil influence from Satan and his followers to draw them away.

And the beat-up and scarred Earth will surely undergo some healing during the Millennial Reign, but then: *When the thousand years come to an end, Satan will be let out of his prison* (Revelation 20:7). I'll do my best to explain why tomorrow.

Day 130

When the thousand years come to an end, Satan will be let out of his prison (Revelation 20:7).

Why, why, why would God choose to do this? The people who will be born on Earth during the Millennial Reign will have had no evil influences to affect their choices. And God isn't interested in creating robots—He wants people to choose to love him.

So in a perfect world, do they? I don't have an answer for that question. I only know that God will allow those who are born during the Millennium free choice just as he has given us. And that means releasing Satan at the end of his Millennial Reign, but only *for a little while* (Revelation 20:3b).

The Bible reminds us over and over that we humans have a naturally sinful nature. Just doing a quick search, I found over a dozen passages referring to man's sinful nature. The Apostle Paul admitted to his own struggle, saying in Romans 7:25b: *In my mind I really want to obey God's law, but because of my sinful nature I am a slave to sin.* Even the Apostle Paul? Yep. But just because his *sinful nature* preferred sin didn't mean Paul had to give in to it. That's why he also said: *Who will free me from this life that is dominated by sin and death? Thank God! The answer is in Jesus Christ our Lord* (Romans 7:24b-25a).

What our *sinful nature* wants us to do can be overcome by calling on the indwelling Holy Spirit—Christ himself—to keep us from giving in to the temptation. Matter of fact, Paul addressed this issue head-on in 1 Corinthians 10:13: *The temptations in your life are no different from what others experience. And God is faithful. He will not allow the temptation to be more than you can stand. When you are tempted, He will show you a way out so that you can endure.*

No one is overpowered by sin except by choice. God provides the *way out*, but it's up to the individual person to either accept that *way out* or stay in the danger zone.

All that said, I still have a hard time with this, but the fact is that the Lord will let Satan *out of his prison*, and *He will go out to deceive the nations—called Gog and Magog—in every corner of the earth* (Revelation 20:8a).

This, I promise, is the devil's last hurrah. Tomorrow we'll see what happens to him and to all who missed out on *the first resurrection* (Revelation 20:5a).

Day 131

When the thousand years come to an end, Satan will be let out of his prison. He will go out to deceive the nations— called Gog and Magog—in every corner of the earth. He will gather them together for battle—a mighty army, as numberless as sand along the seashore. And I saw them as they went up on the broad plain of the earth and surrounded God's people and the beloved city. But fire from heaven came down on the attacking armies and consumed them (Revelation 20:7-9).

Jerusalem, *the beloved city*, will be the location from where Jesus and all his Church, the Bride of Christ, rule over Planet Earth. In Satan's final pathetic attempt, he'll once again find a vast number of people who are willing to throw in their lot with him and help him attack *God's people and the beloved city*.

But no way is the devil going to pull this off. Not one of God's people has to lift a finger. *[F]ire from heaven came down on the attacking armies and consumed them.* And at last, that was that.

Then the devil, who had deceived them, was thrown into the fiery lake of burning sulfur, joining the beast and the false prophet. There they will be tormented day and night forever and ever (Revelation 20:10).

So where's everyone else—all those throughout all time who have rejected Jesus Christ as Lord and Savior? They're apparently roused from their soul sleep (see Day 129 for more about this) or brought out of torment for their final condemnation: *And I saw a great white throne and the one sitting on it. The earth and sky fled from his presence, but they found no place to hide. I saw the dead, both great and small, standing before God's throne. And the books were opened, including the Book of Life. And the dead were judged according to what they had done, as recorded in the books. The sea gave up its dead, and death and the grave gave up their dead. And all were judged according to their deeds. Then death and the grave were thrown into the lake of fire. This lake of fire is the second death. And anyone whose name was not found recorded in the Book of Life was thrown into the lake of fire* (Revelation 20:11-15).

Look at the difference between the resurrection of the saved and the unsaved:

(1) Paul says of the saved: *Our earthly bodies are planted in the ground when we die, but they will be raised to live forever* (1 Corinthians 15:42). Too, there's no waiting period between death and being in the presence of Jesus.

(2) For the lost, they're either in the state called "soul sleep" before being raised for their Final Judgment or else they're already in hell and are only brought out for official sentencing. Only the lost will stand before the Great White Throne of Judgment, and while some believe differently, I hold with those who believe these people will be shown every opportunity they ever had to give their hearts and lives to Jesus. And then their final sentence will be carried out: *[A]nyone whose name was not found recorded in the Book of Life was thrown into the lake of fire.*

The Antichrist, the False Prophet, and the devil and his demons have already been dealt with, and now so has every human being who has rejected Christ's free offer of salvation. What's left to do? Get rid of this messed-up old world and bring in *a new heaven and a new earth* (Revelation 21:1a), which we'll begin exploring tomorrow.

Revelation 21

Day 132

Then I saw a new heaven and a new earth, for the old heaven and the old earth had disappeared. And the sea was also gone (Revelation 21:1).

In 2 Peter 3:13, we read the Apostle Peter's words: *But we are looking forward to the new heavens and new earth he has promised, a world filled with God's righteousness.* Well, brothers and sisters, here it is!

Some Bible scholars claim it's a remake of the Earth and heavens that now exist. Nope, it says right here in today's passage that *the old heaven and the old earth had disappeared.*

And the sea was also gone. Literally? That's another issue for debate, but let me suggest a possibility. In Genesis 1:10 we read: *"God called the dry ground 'land' and the waters 'seas.' And God saw that it was good.* If God himself called this part of his creation *good*, why wouldn't he include it in *the new heavens and new earth*?

In Biblical days, the sea was a place of terror and danger. Sudden storms arose that could take out even the strongest ships. Many men lost their lives working or voyaging on the sea. The *new heaven and ... earth* won't be waterless. Instead, the waters will be beautiful and inviting, safe and serene. There will no longer be any violent, dangerous waters. So perhaps saying *the sea was ... gone* means that all the dangers and unpredictability of the sea will no longer exist.

Take a look at what the prophet Isaiah wrote about this future time: *In that day the wolf and the lamb will live together; the leopard will lie down with the baby goat. The calf and the yearling will be safe with the lion, and a little child will lead them all. The cow will graze near the bear. The cub and the calf will lie down together. The lion will eat hay like a cow. The baby will play safely near the hole of a cobra. Yes, a little child will put its hand in a nest of deadly snakes without harm. Nothing will hurt or destroy in all my holy mountain, for as the waters fill the sea, so the earth will be filled with people who know the Lord* (Isaiah 11:6-9).

If the Lord even allows snakes on the New Earth—something I would prefer he didn't—it would seem that the only thing not included in the New Earth is anything evil or harmful. And what a glorious place to be! *For as the waters fill the sea, so the earth will be filled with people who know the Lord.*

Do you know him, truly know him? If so, you'll be among those who'll spend eternity in this *paradise of God* (Revelation 2:7).

Day 133

Yesterday we got our first glimpse of the new heaven and Earth. Let's look at what else John was shown: *And I saw the holy city, the New Jerusalem, coming down from God out of heaven like a bride beautifully dressed for her husband.*

I heard a loud shout from the throne, saying, 'Look, God's home is now among his people! He will live with them, and they will be his people. God himself will be with them. He will wipe every tear from their eyes, and there will be no more death or sorrow or crying or pain. All these things are gone forever.'

And the one sitting on the throne said, 'Look, I am making everything new!' And then he said to me, 'Write this down, for what I tell you is trustworthy and true' (Revelation 21:2-5).

After all the wars and destruction Jerusalem has experienced, can you even begin to picture the joy John felt to see *the New Jerusalem*! The City of God is revealed, and *God's home is now among His people!*

How many funerals have we attended and heard this promise? *He will wipe every tear from their eyes, and there will be no more death or sorrow or crying or pain.* And this isn't temporary comfort: *All these things are gone forever.* Never again will there be any form of sadness or suffering.

And just to make sure John understood that this was the new forever he and all God's people could look forward to, Jesus speaks from His throne, *Look, I am making everything new!* He even adds, *[W]hat I tell you is trustworthy and true.*

God is so good. He knows we doubt. And instead of chastising us, he reassures us. The Apostle Thomas always gets a bum rap about being a doubter, but let's look at exactly what happened. In John 20, after Jesus' resurrection, he appears to all the disciples except Thomas, who wasn't with the others at that time. Eight days later, Jesus appears to them again, this time with Thomas present. And from this passage, reassuring Thomas seems to be the purpose for this second appearance. Here's the conversation that took place:

Then he said to Thomas, 'Put your finger here, and look at my hands. Put your hand into the wound in my side. Don't be faithless any longer. Believe!'

'My Lord and my God!' Thomas exclaimed.

"Then Jesus told him, 'You believe because you have seen me. Blessed are those who believe without seeing me' (John 20:27-29).

Jesus wasn't chastising Thomas. He simply allowed him the same privilege the other disciples had already experienced: to see him after his resurrection.

Blessed are those who believe without seeing me. That's me and you! We haven't yet seen him face to face, but we know he's God and we know we'll spend eternity with him.

Day 134

And he also said, 'It is finished! I am the Alpha and the Omega—the Beginning and the End. To all who are thirsty I will give freely from the springs of the water of life. All who are victorious will inherit all these blessings, and I will be their God, and they will be my children (Revelation 21:6-7).

Jesus' work is complete. Redeemed mankind's new home is ready. And still Jesus reminds us of his invitation to salvation: *To all who are thirsty I will give freely from the springs of the water of life.* The Water of Life is free—*I will give freely*—but every individual person must choose to accept it.

Let's say you've been outside working in your garden all morning. You come in, hot and thirsty, and there on the countertop in your kitchen sits a Mason jar filled with ice and cool, clear water. You may be fully aware of that water, but it isn't going to do one thing to quench your thirst until you do what? Take it in. Jesus cannot save the person who refuses to take him into their heart.

But for those who do take Jesus into their hearts, they—*[a]ll who are victorious* through faith in Jesus Christ—*will inherit all these blessings, and I will be their God, and they will be my children.* Now that's an offer I can't see anyone choosing to pass up!

But cowards, unbelievers, the corrupt, murderers, the immoral, those who practice witchcraft, idol worshipers, and all liars—their fate is in the fiery lake of burning sulfur. This is the second death (Revelation 21:8).

Another warning, another reminder, of the fate of those who reject the Lordship of Jesus. Most of these are self-explanatory, so I'll only touch on the ones I feel need a bit of clarification:

[C]owards: those who deny Christ when confessing him puts their lives in danger;

[T]hose who practice witchcraft: people who are involved in the use of drugs. Again, this isn't talking about necessary medications, but those drugs that corrupt the mind and spirit. Remember, the Biblical word for *witchcraft* is the same word from which we get our word "pharmacy";

[A]nd all liars: in John 8:44b, Jesus says of Satan, *When he lies, it is consistent with his character; for he is a liar and the father of lies.* Lying is sin. And this sin comes straight from the devil.

But let's not end today on a negative. Let's take a peek at one more verse: *Then one of the seven angels who held the seven bowls containing the seven last plagues came and said to me, 'Come with me! I will show you the bride, the wife of the Lamb'* (Revelation 21:9). We'll get our introduction tomorrow.

Day 135

Then one of the seven angels ... said to me, 'Come with me! I will show you the bride, the wife of the Lamb.' So he took me in the Spirit to a great, high mountain, and he showed me the holy city, Jerusalem, descending out of heaven from God (Revelation 21:9-10).

Hold up a sec! Aren't we the Bride of Christ, those who have accepted Jesus as Lord and Savior? Yes, and this magnificent city will be our home. So in the sense that it will be filled with the people of God, the angel calls it *the wife of the Lamb*. Let's have a look around, shall we?

It shone with the glory of God and sparkled like a precious stone—like jasper as clear as crystal. The city wall was broad and high, with twelve gates guarded by twelve angels. And the names of the twelve tribes of Israel were written on the gates. There were three gates on each side—east, north, south, and west. The wall of the city had twelve foundation stones, and on them were written the names of the twelve apostles of the Lamb (Revelation 21:11-14).

As Kurt Franklin's praise song "Stomp" says, the description of our eternal home "makes me clap my hands, makes me wanna dance!" Our New Jerusalem shines *with the glory of God*. It sparkles *like a precious stone*. And *[t]he city wall* is *broad and high*. Why do we need a wall? That wall does two things: (1) It assures us of the security we have in Jesus; and (2) it reminds us that only those who belong to Jesus belong in that city.

John saw that the wall of New Jerusalem had *twelve gates guarded by twelve angels. And the names of the twelve tribes of Israel were written on the gates. There were three gates on each side—east, north, south, and west.* The *twelve tribes of Israel* are an integral part of the New Jerusalem. The Jews will always have a special place in God's heart, as seen by his special protection over the 144,000 during the Tribulation. (See Revelation 7:4.)

The wall of the city had twelve foundation stones, and on them were written the names of the twelve apostles of the Lamb. The Gospel of Jesus Christ, put forth by his twelve disciples, is the foundation on which the walls of the city stand. This reminds me of Paul's words in Galatians 3:28: *There is no longer Jew or Gentile, slave or free, male and female. For you are all one in Christ Jesus.* In the New Jerusalem, all believers—both Jews and non-Jews—will join together as the family of God.

But there's one more point to ponder here. Who are the *twelve apostles of the Lamb*? We know for certain Judas isn't one of them because Jesus himself calls Judas the *son of destruction* (John 17:12), or "son of perdition" in some translations. So that leaves us with either Matthias (see Acts 1:26), who was chosen to fill the spot vacated by Judas, or Paul, who says in 1 Corinthians 15:9a, *For I am the least of all the apostles.* There is no definite answer, but my vote is for Paul.

Paul was not one of the original twelve disciples chosen by Jesus, but was converted from persecuting the Church to passionately sharing the Good News after his literally blinding encounter with the glorified Jesus as he was traveling the Damascus Road. (See Acts 9). And let's not forget that Paul wrote about half the books of the New Testament.

But we haven't even completed our look around the walls of New Jerusalem. I hope by the time we're finished that we'll all be like Dorothy in "The Wizard of Oz," proclaiming, "There's no place like home!"

Day 136

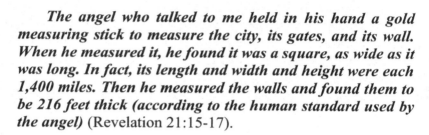

The angel who talked to me held in his hand a gold measuring stick to measure the city, its gates, and its wall. When he measured it, he found it was a square, as wide as it was long. In fact, its length and width and height were each 1,400 miles. Then he measured the walls and found them to be 216 feet thick (according to the human standard used by the angel) (Revelation 21:15-17).

I don't begin to comprehend all this, but if the New Jerusalem is as high as it is wide and long, I'd say we can throw the effects of gravity out the window, because we'll be living in and able to explore the Holy City's entire height, length, and width. And based on the angel's description and measurements, this one city is the size of the Earth's moon, and we're not talking surface space, but, literally, every inch inside and out. Huge. With room enough for all who have and will believe in Jesus.

The wall was made of jasper, and the city was pure gold, as clear as glass. The wall of the city was built on foundation stones inlaid with twelve precious stones: the first was jasper, the second sapphire, the third agate, the fourth emerald, the fifth onyx, the sixth carnelian, the seventh chrysolite, the eighth beryl, the ninth topaz, the tenth chrysoprase, the eleventh jacinth, the twelfth amethyst (Revelation 21:18-20).

Jasper is a type of quartz. The *pure gold* of the city, *as clear as glass*, shows us how the entire city will gleam with the glory of God. And the *twelve precious stones* of the wall's foundations are only a hint of the breathtaking beauty that awaits those who'll live forever in the Holy City.

The twelve gates were made of pearls—each gate from a single pearl! And the main street was pure gold, as clear as glass (Revelation 21:21). All this magnificent architecture can only direct our attention to the Architect. As Ephesians 3:11 reminds us: *This was his eternal plan, which he carried out through Christ Jesus our Lord.* Nothing is random. God's plan has always been at work, and it will be carried out to completion just as the Word of God tells us.

What did Jesus tell his disciples? *There is more than enough room in my Father's home. If this were not so, would I have told you that I am going to prepare a place for you? When everything is ready, I will come and get you, so that you will always be with me where I am* (John 14:2-3).

Ladies and gentlemen, God's house is in order. Is yours?

Day 137

I saw no temple in the city, for the Lord God Almighty and the Lamb are its temple. And the city has no need of sun or moon, for the glory of God illuminates the city, and the Lamb is its light. The nations will walk in its light, and the kings of the world will enter the city in all their glory. Its gates will never be closed at the end of day because there is no night there. And all the nations will bring their glory and honor into the city (Revelation 21:22-26).

I saw no temple in the city, for the Lord God Almighty and the Lamb are its temple. Forget those denominational labels—that won't be happening in the New Jerusalem. Matter of fact, there will be no churches because the real Church, all the redeemed, will be its residents, and we will have open worship of *the Lord God Almighty and the Lamb* all the time, everywhere.

And the city has no need of sun or moon, for the glory of God illuminates the city, and the Lamb is its light. No street lights, no dusk-to-dawns, not even a *sun or moon* because *the glory of God*, who is *the Lamb*, will light the city.

The nations will walk in its light, and the kings of the world will enter the city in all their glory. What *nations*? The nations are the redeemed spoken of in Revelation 5:9: *[F]rom every tribe and language and people and nation.* So what are they doing outside the city? My deep theological answer is: I don't know.

There's a ton of speculation on this, but no definitive answer. Some Bible scholars say the level of rewards given to believers will determine whether they simply live somewhere on the New

Earth or within New Jerusalem. Even if this is so, this doesn't mean a person who is outside the city has received less reward than those inside the city. Some may be delegated as leaders, *kings of the world*, to oversee some of God's people. And all of this is, I repeat, pure speculation.

And what is *all their glory*? In this girl's humble opinion, the only possible glory anyone could have in the New Heaven and Earth is the reflected glory of God. These *kings of the world* have been privileged to help administer the Kingdom of God. That's a huge reward, and that is the only glory I can see these people having.

Its gates will never be closed at the end of day because there is no night there. There is nothing to fear in the New Heaven and Earth. New Jerusalem's gates are *never ... closed* and, as mentioned previously, *the Lamb is its light*. To have unlimited access to the Holy City is to have unlimited access to the Lord.

And all the nations will bring their glory and honor into the city. And as with the kings we've already looked at, the only possible glory anyone could have in the New Heaven and Earth is the reflected glory of God.

Chapter 21 ends with another warning for those who reject Jesus as Lord and Savior: *Nothing evil will be allowed to enter, nor anyone who practices shameful idolatry and dishonesty— but only those whose names are written in the Lamb's Book of Life* (Revelation 21:27).

[O]nly those whose names are written in the Lamb's Book of Life will inhabit the New Heaven and Earth. And there's only one way to get your name into that Book: *Believe in the Lord Jesus and you will be saved* (Acts 16:31a).

Revelation 22

Day 138

Then the angel showed me a river with the water of life, clear as crystal, flowing from the throne of God and of the Lamb. It flowed down the center of the main street. On each side of the river grew a tree of life, bearing twelve crops of fruit, with a fresh crop each month. The leaves were used for medicine to heal the nations (Revelation 22:1-2).

Then the angel showed me a river with the water of life, clear as crystal, flowing from the throne of God and of the Lamb. This may very well be the *sea of glass* (Revelation 4:6 and 15:2) John saw earlier. Its clarity and cleanness exemplify the purifying, *life-giving water* promised in Revelation 7:17.

On each side of the river grew a tree of life, bearing twelve crops of fruit, with a fresh crop each month. In John 15:5, Jesus told his disciples that those who belonged to him would *produce much fruit*. In the New Heaven and Earth, those who have borne much fruit for the Kingdom will have full access to the *tree of life* and enjoy its continual offerings.

The leaves were used for medicine to heal the nations. No one is sick or in sin in the New Heaven and Earth. The word written as *heal* is better understood as "providing health." Whether this reference is figurative or literal, we can be certain that there will be no form of sickness in the New Heaven and Earth.

No longer will there be a curse upon anything. For the throne of God and of the Lamb will be there, and his servants will worship him. And they will see his face, and his name will be written on their foreheads. And there will be no night there— no need for lamps or sun—for the Lord God will shine on them. And they will reign forever and ever (Revelation 22:3-5).

No longer will there be a curse upon anything. When Adam and Eve sinned, they were cast from the Garden of Eden and the curse of sin came into the world. In our eternal home, there'll be no curse.

For the throne of God and of the Lamb will be there, and his servants will worship him. And they will see his face, and his name will be written on their foreheads. And there will be no night there—no need for lamps or sun—for the Lord God will shine on them. In our eternal home, we'll see the very face of our Savior. We'll bear his name, and the only light we'll ever need is Jesus.

And they will reign forever and ever. No more evil. Only joy and peace forever. I'm so thankful I'll get to be there. Are you excited about your eternal home?

Day 139

'Look, I am coming soon! Blessed are those who obey the words of prophecy written in this book.'

I, John, am the one who heard and saw all these things. And when I heard and saw them, I fell down to worship at the feet of the angel who showed them to me. But he said, 'No, don't worship me. I am a servant of God, just like you and your brothers the prophets, as well as all who obey what is written in this book. Worship only God!'

"Then he instructed me, 'Do not seal up the prophetic words in this book, for the time is near (Revelation 22:7-10).

Jesus' words open this portion of the final chapter of Revelation. *Look, I am coming soon!* As we saw at the beginning of this study, the word translated *soon* is actually a word that I can best explain as meaning when it happens, it will happen in a split second. Nothing about Christ's plan has changed or been delayed. He is ready to call his Church home the very moment the Father gives the command.

We also see here the same passage about John being so overwhelmed by all he sees and hears that he starts to fall to his knees in front of an angel. This is simply another reminder that angels are created beings and they are never to be worshiped or prayed to. They are just as the angel told John, servants of God with no power or authority except what is given them by their Creator.

Then he instructed me, 'Do not seal up the prophetic words in this book, for the time is near. The Lord doesn't want us to fear or ignore the Book of Revelation. We need to study it and be prepared for when Jesus calls his Church out of this world. The time is very ***near***, and you can take that to the bank.

But look how long ago John wrote down the Revelation, and it hasn't happened yet. Second Peter 3:8 says: ***But you must not forget this one thing, dear friends: A day is like a thousand years to the Lord, and a thousand years is like a day.*** God's plan will be carried out, and the countless prophecies leading up to this time that have already been fulfilled are obvious indicators of the nearness of Christ's return. You have two urgent missions: (1) be ready; and (2) prepare others.

Day 140

Let the one who is doing harm continue to do harm; let the one who is vile continue to be vile; let the one who is righteous continue to live righteously; let the one who is holy continue to be holy (Revelation 22:11).

Don't misunderstand this passage, because it's referring to the imminence of the Rapture. When Christ calls out the Church, anyone who doesn't belong to Jesus will be left behind. Those who are his children will be headed for glory.

'Look, I am coming soon, bringing my reward with me to repay all people according to their deeds (Revelation 22:12). The unrighteous, the unsaved, have already been dealt with, so this statement refers to the rewards the faithful will receive in glory. Yes, every person who has accepted Jesus Christ as Lord and Savior will be in heaven, and every person will be rewarded *according to their deeds*.

I am the Alpha and the Omega, the First and the Last, the Beginning and the End (Revelation 22:13). Jesus spoke this world into being, and this world will be removed and the New Heaven and Earth ushered in at his command.

Blessed are those who wash their robes. They will be permitted to enter through the gates of the city and eat the fruit from the tree of life (Revelation 22:14). Robes are given by the Bridegroom to those who are a part of the Wedding Celebration, and all who are there have been washed in the blood of the Lamb. And the Holy City's *gates will never be closed* (Revelation 21:25a).

Outside the city are the dogs—the sorcerers, the sexually immoral, the murderers, the idol worshipers, and all who love to live a lie (Revelation 22:15). Are these evildoers literally right *[o]utside the city*? No, the New Heaven and Earth is a sinless, perfect Paradise. Galatians 5:21b makes it plain that *people who do these kinds of things will not inherit the kingdom of God* (GNT). This is simply a way of reminding those who have yet to turn to Jesus that they'll miss out on all the wonders of the Eternal Kingdom of God.

It grieves my heart to think of anyone missing out on the New Heaven and Earth, and I hope it does yours as well. Do your part to share the Good News and point others to Jesus.

Day 141

'I, Jesus, have sent my angel to give you this testimony for the churches. I am the Root and the Offspring of David, the bright Morning Star.'

The Spirit and the bride say, 'Come!' Let the one who hears say, 'Come!' And let the one who is thirsty come, and the one who desires the water of life drink freely.

I testify to everyone who hears the words of prophecy in this book: If anyone adds to them, God will add to him the plagues described in this book. And if anyone takes away from the words of this book of prophecy, God will take away his share in the tree of life and in the holy city, which are described in this book.

He who testifies to these things says, 'Yes, I am coming soon.' Amen. Come, Lord Jesus! The grace of the Lord Jesus be with all the saints. Amen (Revelation 22:16-21, BSB).

These are the final words of the Book of Revelation. Jesus himself speaks twice in this closing passage: (1) *I, Jesus, have sent my angel to give you this testimony for the churches. I am the Root and the Offspring of David, the bright Morning Star*; and (2) *Yes, I am coming soon.* There can be no doubt that this book, like every book in the Bible, is the irrefutable Word of God.

The hour is late, but the invitation continues, *Come!* And who is extending this invitation? *The Spirit and the bride.* We, brothers and sisters, as *the bride*, through the power of the indwelling Holy Spirit, are to be about God's business, inviting others into the Kingdom before it's too late.

Finally, we see the stern warning that has frightened so many people away from the Book of Revelation: *I testify to everyone who hears the words of prophecy in this book: If anyone adds to them, God will add to him the plagues described in this book. And if anyone takes away from the words of this book of prophecy, God will take away his share in the tree of life and in the holy city, which are described in this book.*

Exactly what does this mean? Don't corrupt the Scriptures—any of them, although this warning pertains specifically to the Book of Revelation. Be as careful as possible in interpreting what you read, and always be willing to say, "I don't know," or "I'm not sure." Most of all, this warning is to all scribes and Bible translators throughout the ages not to add or remove anything from what was written in the original message given to John.

He who testifies to these things says, 'Yes, I am coming soon.' Amen. Come, Lord Jesus! The grace of the Lord Jesus be with all the saints. Amen.

It's true, it's all true, and Jesus' return is on the horizon. Are you ready? To whom are you explaining the urgency?

I hope you've enjoyed our walk through Revelation and that you've become much more comfortable with reading and studying it. God bless each and every one of you.

My Testimony

I grew up in a Christian home. My mom sang in the choir, taught Sunday school, and worked with our church's women's organization. My dad sang in the choir, was the bass in the church quartet, and served in a number of capacities around the church. My sister and I grew up playing with the preacher's kids at the parsonage next door to the church; doing homework on church pews during choir practice and business meetings; and participating in every children's program the church offered.

So on the Sunday when, during the invitation, my dad walked down the aisle and told our pastor that he needed to be saved and baptized, this 10-year-old Daddy's girl shot down the aisle right behind him. I was sprinkled, prayed over, and put on the church roll as a member.

Years later, I married my husband Larry. We began attending my church, but Larry's roots drew us to a Baptist church where, when we decided to move our membership, I was told my "sprinkling" baptism wasn't acceptable for church membership. So I submitted to baptism by emersion.

Two baptisms—sprinkling and emersion—and I can assure you that neither one of them "took." But I was busy in the church. I was even teaching a children's Sunday school class. Larry and I had just built a new home, had a precious baby boy, and a wonderful life.

Which is why it was so hard for me to understand why I still felt like something was missing. One night that restlessness drove me from our bed and into the living room where I sat in the dark and prayed and pondered what was wrong with me. I can only say that during that time of prayer, I truly met the Lord. I realized I'd been going through all the motions, but I'd never truly asked Jesus

Christ to be the Lord of my life. That night changed my life. That night changed my eternity.

The following Sunday, I could hardly wait for our pastor to finish his sermon, I was so eager to walk that aisle and ask for real believer's baptism. I let the whole church know I'd put the cart before the horse and that I wanted to be baptized as a true born-again Christian.

And as the old saying goes, the third time was a charm. My third baptism was in the proper order: salvation first, then baptism.

There's no embarrassment in admitting you're unsure of your salvation. And there's wonderful peace and security in knowing that you know that you know. If you have any doubts, talk to your pastor. Talk to a strong Christian friend. But get things right with the Lord. Time is short, and I don't want anyone missing out on the grand eternity awaiting all of Jesus' children.

Where to Find Me

You can read my daily Bible posts, bargains, and more by visiting my Facebook page—just search for the word Bargainomics—and by visiting my website, www.Bargainomics.com. You can also follow me on Twitter and receive short messages of encouragement.